EVERYWHERE

THE UNDROWNED

GREAT CIRCLE BOOKS

Kiese Laymon and Marie Mutsuki Mockett,
EDITORS

———

EDITORIAL BOARD

Rosalind Bentley

Barrie Jean Borich

Stephanie Elizondo Griest

Randon Billings Noble

Hasanthika Sirisena

John Jeremiah Sullivan

ADVISORY MEMBERS

Sayantani Dasgupta

Megha Majumdar

Great Circle Books publishes literary nonfiction—including memoir, literary journalism, personal and lyric essays, and work that defies easy classification—by emerging writers. The Great Circle is the intersection of lines on the celestial sphere—lines overlapping and creating new entryways of understanding. In that spirit, Great Circle Books seeks, through innovative work, to merge the human experience with our relationship to place.

A complete list of books published in Great Circle Books is available at https://uncpress.org/series/great-circle-books.

STEPHANIE CLARE SMITH

Everywhere

the

Undrowned

A MEMOIR
OF SURVIVAL AND
IMAGINATION

The University of North Carolina Press
CHAPEL HILL

Designed and typeset by Lindsay Starr
Set in Iowan Old Style

Cover art: *Though They May Be Unglittering*
(photo © Robynne Limoges, www.robynnelimoges.com)

LIBRARY OF CONGRESS CATALOGING-IN-PUBLICATION DATA
Names: Smith, Stephanie Clare, author.
Title: Everywhere the undrowned : a memoir of survival
and imagination / Stephanie Clare Smith.
Other titles: Great circle books.
Description: Chapel Hill :
The University of North Carolina Press, 2024. |
Series: Great circle books
Identifiers: LCCN 2023034115 |
ISBN 9781469678962 (paperback ; alk. paper) |
ISBN 9781469678979 (ebook)
Subjects: LCSH: Smith, Stephanie Clare—Childhood and youth. |
Teenage girls—Louisiana—New Orleans—Biography. | Adult child abuse
victims—Biography. | Mothers and daughters—Louisiana—New Orleans. |
Child abuse—Psychological aspects. | Mediators (Persons)—Biography. |
LCGFT: Creative nonfiction. | Autobiographies.
Classification: LCC HQ798 .S586 2024 |
DDC 306.874—dc23/eng/20230830
LC record available at https://lccn.loc.gov/2023034115

Excerpt from Jean Valentine's "In prison," from *Break the Glass*,
was originally published in the *New Yorker*, May 27, 2007.
Copyright © 2007, 2010 by Jean Valentine. Reprinted with
the permission of The Permissions Company, LLC, on behalf
of Copper Canyon Press, coppercanyonpress.org.

The song "We Belong to a Mutual Admiration Society,"
lyrics by Matt Dubey, music by Harold Karr © 1955
(renewed) Chappell & Co., Inc. All rights reserved.
Used by permission of Alfred Music.

For Jeanette, the right one to trust

you
who the earth was for.

—JEAN VALENTINE

EVERYWHERE
THE UNDROWNED

Part I

Poets can do whatever they want. . . . I started a
practice of creating rituals to maintain a presence
so that I could only be where I was.

—CACONRAD

TO HAVE LESS THAN NOTHING, they created algebra. They
made me take it twice.

Four of us sat at a round table in the junior high school library—
an algebra do-over in the heat of a New Orleans summer. A 100
percent humidity 100 percent of the time summer. Our forearms
stuck to the textbooks, the round table, the mimeographed work-
sheets. We each brought a washcloth from home to wipe away our
sweat. Mr. Martin was one of the nicest teachers around. During
the school year he taught civics and history, but the principal had
him teach algebra all summer long. Mr. Martin made a dot on the
green board and labeled it *A*. Then he erased the dot and the *A* and
told us it was still there.

Each night that summer I chose a book from the bookshelf in the
living room of our apartment and laid it on the table by my bed—a
talisman of sorts. *Autobiography of a Yogi* was a frequent visitor. I'd
skim the pages to randomly pick out words that caught my eye—
swami, immeasurably uplifted, soul-life, amulet. My real talisman was
Jane Eyre, the book I actually read and reread—an amulet of sorts.
Jane was eighteen, out wandering the moors, and I was fourteen,
riding on streetcars.

OUR APARTMENT was on the second floor of a gray stucco four-plex one block away from Loyola University, where everyone was smart. The only other kids in the neighborhood were the ones in uniform driven in each morning to attend Holy Name of Jesus primary school. The school sat right across from our fourplex. The school sat empty all summer long. Holy Name installed a silver chain-link fence around its parochial playground and topped it with rows of barbed wire to keep the rest of us out. My junior high was thirteen blocks away.

I didn't need a nightlight those nights. I had a home full of lights. One lamp stayed up with me each night and burned through the dark hours like a god—a god reduced to one believer.

I remember not knowing the other tenants in our building. They were mostly grad students who came and went like everyone else in our neighborhood, and there was one who was scary. He got in loud fights and had lost part of his hand in some kind of accident. On the weekends, he shot at the stray dogs and cats that roamed through our street.

There was another scary neighbor who lived in the ground floor apartment of the raised duplex behind us. The dark rooms with short ceilings and cement floors are what we call a basement in our city below sea level. If you peered through this neighbor's dirty windows you'd see a maze of newspapers stacked five feet high and one unmade skinny bed in the back of the room. The neighbor threatened to kill anyone who came poking around looking in the windows of his basement apartment. I did only once.

There is a black-and-white photograph of my mother from before I was born. From when she had just met my father. I found it at the bottom of a box filled with school photos and baby pictures. She's standing outside dressed in blue jeans and a dark blouse with small white polka dots looking for all the world like the actor Suzanne Pleshette. She looks happy, covered in stars that complement her curly black hair. Not the kind of person to be afraid at night.

When I was five years old, before my father left, he bought our first television set. We gathered on the brown braided rug by the black-and-white fire. Our favorites were *Wild Kingdom* and *I've Got a Secret*. An antelope on a plain in Africa was murdered by lions in front of us. There was lots of gray blood, but I knew it was red. At the end of a break for station identification, our front door banged open and two girls, older than me, ran in, big-eyed.

A man, or something, is after us. They tried not to cry. One was holding a stone. One had mud on her knees. My mother turned off the dead antelope and my father drove the girls home in his white station wagon. I stared into the trees through my dark window face, big-eyed and pounding.

~~

EVEN ALGEBRA was softer in the summer, curly. Even our textbooks took pity on us and wilted a little. There was one fan in the room—the kind that didn't oscillate. We took turns orbiting it with our washcloths.

Mostly, white kids went to other schools. I was in the 10 percent who didn't go to private schools, or Catholic schools, or the one public school for supersmart kids who took an IQ test in order to get in. I wondered if those kids ever went to summer school, and if they did, were their summer school rooms full of air-conditioned air.

I didn't understand what humidity really was until years later when I left New Orleans. Other towns were hot during the summer, but their summers didn't swell into other months and their air didn't swell so thick that each breath felt like you were trying to inhale a couch cushion.

You wouldn't be wrong to say that algebra comes from zero. That's what my summer school teacher told me. Zero is a portal of sorts, made famous by Brahmagupta, an Indian mathematician and astronomer. On one side of zero, the positive numbers march forward into endless space. On the other side, the negative numbers march backward into endless space.

3

In mathematics, zero equals the lack of something and division equals the breaking apart of something. Every number can be broken apart, except for zero. Breaking apart zero makes no sense.

Mr. Martin drew a zero in the middle of the board. Then he added a long line on both sides and asked me to come up and draw a car at ground zero. I drew a circle with four little zero wheels. I drew windows and doors and labeled it VW. Mr. Martin had a story about the car driving west into the negative numbers of Texas and east into the positive numbers of Mississippi all to show me why multiplying two negative numbers creates a positive answer. I was lost on the highway, but no one could tell.

Everything is easier to set aside when it's smaller, close to zero, where the possibilities are endless and sometimes mysterious. And if all else fails, you can always count on zero.

～～

I REMEMBER swimming with my mother when I was younger. If we were at a hotel or the community pool, and if I pleaded with her enough at just the right time, she would let me hold her shoulders while she swam parallel a foot or so below me underwater. She'd pull us through the blue pool in a long glide, my head just above the chlorinated surface. Her arms like wings below me revealed a kind of angel-seal hybrid. But then she'd go too deep, and I would have to decide—let go or hold my breath and try to follow her under. Sometimes she was tired of me holding on. Sometimes she was just a wild seal.

One year, my mother sewed covers for all my schoolbooks from fabric she knew had more life to give. A striped mattress cover covered Spelling. History sported her blue corduroy jacket, while English showed off red pedal pushers. I loved all the textures of her remnants.

I remember a night in December when *The Messiah* brought down the junior high house. We all made our way out of the school auditorium and into the night with Handel humming through us.

Clusters of people milled about on the sidewalk. The ninth-grade choir and the rest of my peers glided away with parents to parties. Car doors slammed, engines turned over, and then it was just me, milling in the dark waiting for my mother, who had said she'd be there to pick me up at the end. After a while, I moved into the night shadows under the wide oaks at the back of the building, where I could stay hidden. No one could see inside of me there. I watched the custodians shut down the school and leave it behind. The blackout got blacker. I never thought to ask them for help. She never liked to be called out.

My mother told me that I was the kind of kid who was psychic with her, but I wasn't sure what she was talking about. The Amazing Kreskin said he wasn't really psychic either. He just knew how to read people's micro-expressions. All I did was get up every morning and pay attention.

Pretend I'm not home, she'd say when she was busy at home writing bills or sorting papers or talking with a friend. But I was the one pretended away. When my mother went out for the night, I'd imagine her into the living room with me. I'd make a stack of cinnamon toast for us both, shout out a joke, and invent her response.

I used to see molecules—millions floating everywhere. Trees breathe in what we breathe out. I'd hold my breath that could be full of Lincoln's air, Sir Francis Drake, Nefertiti. All these people lived right here. No one's ever really over.

Turns out the molecules are *neurological noise* in my field of vision. For 10 percent, the noise is normal—a visual snow syndrome you can see right through.

Normal were the many nights I counted cars that came and went that were not hers. Their lights would sail around my room like the prayers I spun to bring her home. I loved the sounds when she returned—her tambourine of keys at the door, her steps riffing into the kitchen. Jazzy smoke would loop through my room, and all the world settled down.

When my mother lectured me and I didn't understand what she was saying, she would make me take her obese dictionary off the bottom shelf of the bookcase and look up the words that had gone over my head. I would get lost in the etymology of the word or the obsolete definitions or the list of synonyms and antonyms I found there. I would try to figure out which definition fit in with her arguments. I would not get any closer to understanding the lecture, but I did get closer to words.

My mother liked how I paid attention. She liked the letters I wrote to presidents starting when I was eight years old.

Dear LBJ,
  Please end the war.

My mother was a freelance modern dancer. The city's recreation department hired her to teach modern dance in the public schools. The early definitions of *dance* meant to move quickly and impulsively, sometimes erratically. Everyone loved how my mother could move.

My favorite color has always been green—same for my mother. She was full-on green, the lucky shade of green, shamrock green, the verdant green of life on earth. She was a shimmering green dress set off by her black curls, sky-blue eyes, and red swoosh of lipstick going out on a date.

If you saw my mother's boyfriend back then with his salt-and-pepper beard and his black horn-rimmed glasses, you might've thought he was a jazz musician. If he had been a jazz musician back then, he might've been a bebop drummer in a quartet that no one ever heard of. Instead, my mother's boyfriend was an under-employed freelance photographer that no one ever heard of. He liked to talk about how cameras work, how the eyes work. How images come in upside down first, how our brains and our cameras flip them back around to normal and capture the important moments in our big and little histories. How everything depends on the light we absorb.

IN SCIENCE, a color is a wavelength of visible light. You would be wrong to think of white light as zero color or the absence of color. Instead, it's the color wheel spun so quickly that the colors dance into a white haze of all colors, all possible colors before the refraction.

My nights were mostly a gray wavelength—*Gunsmoke* gray, our Calhoun Street apartment gray when my mother was not home, gray like the black-and-white Sony TV that kept me company at night. I was glued to the shows that starred someone else left on their own, our landscapes the same at least for an hour. I scanned every black-and-white moment for the lessons they learned.

Tony Curtis played Harry Houdini on channel 6 late one night. He could escape any box with a lock, but he couldn't find his mother no matter what he did. No séance seemed to work, so there was no way to reach her. But then, when Houdini was trapped under the ice in a frozen river during an escape-artist trick gone wrong, his mother's *soul-life* called his name and led him back to the hole in the ice. Some mothers are dead and still stick around.

In our Calhoun Street apartment, when *Gunsmoke* came on, I waited for Kitty, who ran the saloon. She stole every scene the way she stayed clean and curly while the men turned to dirt. But sometimes Kitty never showed up. Sometimes the whole night was the color of cowboys—unkind and unkempt.

BEFORE MY mother's boyfriend attended a single AA meeting, before he got to the fourth step and made a *searching and fearless inventory* of himself, before he relapsed and died, he drank a fifth of whiskey every night.

But all I really understood back then was that I preferred him in the daytime when he would talk about things like books and cameras and the Watergate crimes. At night he would chain-smoke and talk too long and too loud and argue with everyone and not listen to anyone and drop lit cigarettes on the floor and need to be tended to by my mother. She'd stay out with him most nights and come home way after I was in bed. And once she left our apartment door wide open after coming home late and the cops showed up with guns drawn and flashlights everywhere, certain we were under attack, because no one leaves their apartment door wide open in New Orleans no matter what neighborhood they live in. And I woke up right away and she didn't wake up, even with the cops standing in her room and shining lights in her face, until they made me rouse her. Things like that seemed to happen a lot.

My mother envied the astronauts. She was not the kind of person to be afraid of flying to the moon. She often told me and her boyfriend how much she wished she could sit in a rocket and fly into the sky. How she would have been one of those early explorers setting out across an ocean hundreds of years ago when everyone else thought the world was still flat. But now she wanted to fly into new outer space worlds with danger for fuel.

I wanted to tell her that danger is overrated. That zooming up into the sky and flying there alone is not exciting. I wanted to tell her that I would never leave the earth, but she already knew that. She definitely knew that.

What she really wanted us to know was how lucky we were she didn't have a rocket.

〜〜

MOST OF the houses in New Orleans are built a few feet off the ground—ready for floods. Stray cats and dogs take shelter there from the pouring-down rain and the pouring-down sun. I left a handful of scraps every morning under our building, just in case my pet cat was hanging around there and afraid to come out.

I had trained her with cheese and bits of shrimp to come when I called her, and it worked. She'd come running the way a pet dog comes running for a treat or a tennis ball, except my cat was quiet like a fox or a cloud. She'd glide over the rooftops of the neighbors' sheds or scoot out from underneath the dark gap of one of the houses.

My mother had let me pick her out from the box of *Free Kittens* right before my eleventh birthday. I named her Napoleon after the avenue my mother's boyfriend lived on and because we were reading about Napoleon in history class that year. I named her Napoleon before I knew she was a she, before she got pregnant at ten months old and then lost all of her kittens because she was too young to be pregnant and my mother said cats don't need to go to doctors anyway. After she had kittens, I called her Napper instead. My mother liked Napper better when Napper was outside.

Cats heal themselves, my mother said when Napper was tumbled under a car and came limping home, and I asked if we could please please take her to a veterinarian's office. Napper's limp mostly faded after a few months, but I could still see it. She'd hang her bad leg over the edge of the step or the table or whatever she was sitting on because it still hurt.

Cats don't get sad, my mother said the next year when I told her that Napper was depressed. *She's only three. She has nothing to be sad about*, my mother said. Still, I could see it.

That's what cats do when they are ready to die, my mother said when Napper didn't come home after a week of being sad. I called her name every morning from the back porch and all the way down the street as I walked to school. For months, I left her food under our fourplex and the house next door, just in case she wasn't ready to die. In my mind's eye, I could see her so clearly.

The food was always gone when I got home, but I knew it was the birds, the flurry of sparrows that waited for me each morning. They would cha-cha around me and fight with each other. I would have named them all as though they were pets, but they were never still long enough for something like names.

~~~

IF YOU could get a ride across Lake Pontchartrain or to one of the cow fields out by the airport in Kenner, and if there had been a hard rain the day before, and if you knew how to identify psilocybin mushrooms, they were free for the picking. Cow patties plus

9

rain plus Louisiana couch-cushion humidity equals magic mushroom soul-life.

Sometimes my friend Julie could find us a ride. Other times she didn't mind hitchhiking. Whenever we hitched a ride anywhere, I sat in the back seat holding the door handle. I wanted to be more like Julie—less full of worry and more ready to go, but I had a bad feeling whenever we hitchhiked, a kind of flash forward, a very gray feeling.

Don't be scared. Don't be scared.

Later, we come to use terms like *post-traumatic stress disorder,* words like *survivor.* Later, I will read about medical researchers exploring the benefits of microdoses of psilocybin on post-traumatic stress disorder and I will remember the secret life of mushrooms and the way I felt *immeasurably uplifted.*

～～

THE TEACHERS in summer school started bringing washcloths to class, too. Ours were bright colors—orange, aqua, lime green with zigzags or stripes on them. When you weren't using them to wipe sweat from your face, you folded them into your back pocket so the top was just tipping over the edge of your pocket. It was a Deep South kind of summer school fashion statement. Most of the teachers' washcloths were plain white or beige washcloths, which they kept out of sight in their desk drawer or cupboard most of the time, except for Mr. Martin. His washcloth was a thin yellow cloth with a border full of smiling blue ducks. He didn't care that we teased him when he walked down the hall with the row of ducks bouncing over the edge of his back pocket.

It's my baby son's washcloth, he finally told us. *Perfect size. Much more practical than the ones you all carry.*

Mr. Martin soaked his son's washcloth in ice water from the teacher's lounge every morning and then held it to his neck as he sat down at the round table in the library with us. Water dripped down his neck and arm. Once he started talking about numbers, he forgot the heat, forgot his washcloth on his chair, and was deep in his number zone. He sweated through his undershirt and short-sleeve dress shirt in the first thirty minutes.

Numbers are everywhere. You can do anything with numbers.

I told Mr. Martin that I thought zero was both nothing and something all at the same time. Mr. Martin looked at me for a while. *It's not that you are wrong . . .*

Wrong = not right. So, I am not not right.

. . . but let's make sure you know how to multiply and divide negative numbers and solve for x first.

At the round table we complained to Mr. Martin about how much math there was to learn, how it kept changing like some kind of trick. How if we ever passed Algebra 1, there was Geometry 1 waiting and then Algebra 2. Mr. Martin filled the green board with Roman numerals.

That's what happens if things don't change. You are stuck with a clunky way of figuring things out. Just remember, numbers can do anything if you can find the right ones.

My favorite number was eight. Eight looked like infinity standing on its head.

And after listening to Mr. Martin, I had also become a fan of zero.

But is zero a number? I asked.

In 1973, the NFL had decided it wasn't—at least not on jerseys. *Zero is too confusing,* they said.

Mr. Martin pointed at the number line on the board with my VW zero sitting in the middle. *If you can find zero, then isn't it a number?*

Mr. Martin asked me. I wanted to remind him that I had failed algebra the first time, so it wasn't likely that I could answer his trick question. But he didn't believe that we had failed. He said we just didn't realize how much we knew.

Even the NFL let the players already wearing zero and double zero keep their numbers until they retired.

I wanted to stay in my summer school circle where Mr. Martin believed the four of us failed subjects were smarter than we were. A chapter in my ninth-grade science book explained that everything is relative and space is endless. That neither the beginning nor the center nor the east nor the west of space can be found. The chapter included a helpful illustration—a boy stood outside of his house at night pointing a flashlight up into the dark sky. The caption explained that unless the beam of light hit a cloud or a star or space rocks floating around in the universe, it could, in theory, travel the universe forever without being absorbed.

Negative numbers and zero aren't things we can touch or hold, Mr. Martin said. *But their creation was a useful fiction for certain ways of relating. Instead of saying, I owe you 30 dollars, I can use numbers and write negative thirty and we all know what I'm lacking.*

This is a story of certain relationships and useful fiction.

Part 2

There is an invisible world all around you.
A kingdom of spirits commissioned to guard you,
Jane. Do you not see them?

—HELEN BURNS IN THE FILM *JANE EYRE*

I LIKED TO WATCH the moon rise outside of my window like a silver bubble in a dark aquarium. I liked to imagine other people near and far looking up at our moon at the very same time. I'd think of Apollo 11 and the ticker-tape parade I saw when I visited my father, who was in Houston that summer. I only had eyes for Michael and Buzz. The whole world had eyes for Neil.

The reporters would only ever have one real question for Michael Collins—the question that wouldn't go away. Was he scared floating around to the dark side of the moon all by himself? And he would answer the question the same way his whole life. He wasn't all that scared of the dark. He was scared the mission would fail, and he'd have to leave his two colleagues behind.

Sometime during that visit in Houston, I bought postcards of the first photos of Earth from the moon. Sometime that summer I wrote a poem for Senator Eugene McCarthy, who was a poet from Minnesota. Poets can do whatever they want, and he wanted to be president and end the war. They called him Clean Gene. After he lost the Democratic nomination, I sent him the poem I'd written. He wrote me back and I kept the letter forever, so I could absorb all his good words.

EUGENE J. McCARTHY
MINNESOTA

𝔘nited 𝔖tates 𝔖enate

WASHINGTON, D.C.

October 13, 1969

Miss Stephanie Smith
1907 Calhoun Street
New Orleans, Louisiana 70118

Dear Stephanie:

I appreciate your sending me a copy of the poem which you wrote. I am enclosing one of my poems.

Also enclosed is the information you requested on air pollution.

With best wishes.

Sincerely yours,

Eugene J. McCarthy

EJM:gc
encs.

I took postcards I'd saved of

    the planet Earth in the night sky

    a ruined pyramid in Mexico somewhere

    Ling-Ling and Hsing-Hsing, the new giant panda
        bears at the Smithsonian Zoo

    Van Gogh's *Starry Night*

and put them in different kitchen cabinets. That way, when I reached for a glass or a plate or the box of Cheerios, I'd get a surprise. Like windows. Like a group of friends eager to see me with stories to tell.

On cloudless nights, I stood on our back porch where there was just enough room for a washing machine and a clothesline. I held my flashlight over whatever still-damp clothes I'd hung out earlier in the thick, damp day and shined a beam through the humid atmosphere into the black space, just like the boy in my science book had. I aimed as carefully as I could between the stars. There was a chance that beam of light would travel forever. I flashed the light off and on in my own made-up Morse code, just in case it spelled out who I was. Just in case someone in some world was on their back porch and would look up and read me.

Every night, I looked for the first star to show up in the darkening sky. Then I would put my hand on my heart and feel it beating. I would say *Tecumseh* out loud. Tecumseh was a Shawnee leader, and his name meant "shooting star." I read all about his life in a book I found called *The Patriot Chiefs*, by Alvin Josephy Jr. I read about how loyal Tecumseh was. How he spent his life trying to unite the tribes into a kind of confederacy so they could win. How he was killed in the War of 1812 on October 5th, my birthday. Of course, he died 146 years before I was born, but still, it was something.

Maybe some people's stories are like a light traveling all the way through space until they make contact with something and are absorbed. Maybe people name towns and buildings and ships after their heroes with the hope that they will absorb their good hero parts. I wanted to absorb Tecumseh's confederacy, his brave banners flying in the wind, and I figured it would take more than just knowing his name and being born on the anniversary of the day he was killed to make this happen. I figured a ritual with the night's first starlight and my heartbeat and his name would make a fine show. One he would appreciate. One that might just bring a little absorption. It wouldn't hurt to try.

There's a smile on my face for the whole human race. Why, it's almost like being in love.—Lerner and Loewe

This is a love story. Or at least a close synonym.

～～

THAT SUMMER school summer, my mother set me to the side for five or six weeks—me on my own in our fourplex apartment with algebra homework, my eighteen-year-old brother out of the house, my little sister off with our father. My mother and her boyfriend were traveling out west, camping somewhere, across half the country. I knew the probability of her calling me from a campground was mathematically insignificant.

I carried her suitcase to her silver Honda Z. The tiny car had two cylinders and two doors and was the kind of car four men could pick up, the kind that ranked first in gas mileage during the 1973 OPEC oil crisis, the kind of car that looked like a circus prop that twelve clowns would collapse into and drive around in circles while elephants pretended to dance on a stage. I put her suitcase next to his suitcase. Their tent, two sleeping bags, their snacks and maps and binoculars and cameras were all collapsed together in the back seat, all part of her summer disappearing act.

I remember asking my mother not to go on her trip. We stood in the living room on the green shag rug. Her favorite abstract painting hung on the wall over her shoulder—a pale-blue still life with unconventional lemons spilled across a square table. In our mini-aquarium, the pair of small African frogs came up for air and floated on the surface among all the bubbles while I readied myself to just ask her to stay or else take me along with her.

Asking was like attempting a U-turn on the high dive ladder at the community pool. Everyone cringes as you climb down the ladder. You think you want solid ground under your feet, but it's better to just get it over with and jump in the damn water. The sting of hitting the water is just a fast slap in the face, and shame looks better underwater anyway.

You'll be fine. She rolled her eyes. *Teenagers love being on their own . . . you'll see.* Then she smiled. *You won't even want me to come back.* I stared at her suitcase and nodded.

At school, I discovered that if you blink your eyes when something moves in front of you, and if you keep your eyes shut for few seconds after you blink, you will see its afterimage. It gets captured, sealed inside somewhere—the place where what we see comes in and stays. Master Kan on the TV show *Kung Fu* said that the objects the eyes see disappear. But what the soul sees stays forever.

My mother didn't know that I wrote my name and my favorite number eight in black Magic Marker on the bottom of her shoes before she took off. She couldn't see my name on the black soles, but it was there, touching the ground with her, wherever she was, around, somewhere. I may not have had a number to reach her, but I was sure she could feel me.

The silver flash of car, her hand leaning out of the driver's window, her moonstone ring catching the light as she waved goodbye.

～～

FIRST, I tried naming the knives in the kitchen after the kids I babysat for—Cathy, Bill, Todd, Maggie. But still they looked dangerous—ready to defect with the first intruder who broke through the little lock on the apartment's front door. Even loyal, one slip through tomato pulp to the thumb bone and who will fix this all-alone mess? Who will drive this mess to the hospital?

Not having an insurance card equals having no insurance. Hospitals require someone who can sign for things.

So, I hid the knives—boys under the stove, girls in the freezer.

The lock on the front door of the apartment was the simple kind, the twist button in the middle of the doorknob kind. The kind you can open with a butter knife in the keyhole or a school ID card pressed between the lock and the door. The back door had the serious kind of lock, the dead bolt kind. I was a fan of that dead bolt.

Laura Petrie improvised a makeshift alarm system on the *Dick Van Dyke Show*. She was a mother in her thirties and still she was scared when home alone for one night. So, she piled pots and pans in front of the door. That way, if someone broke the lock and opened the door she would hear the crash and be able to get a head start. She was babysitting the neighbor's pet parrot and the parrot kept saying—*Don't be scared. Don't be scared.*

I was groomed for the task of Don't Be Scared. I learned Don't Be Scared the way free divers learn Don't Breathe In as they swim headfirst into the blue-black sea with only a wet suit and a face mask. No tank of air is strapped to their backs. No nothing but the air they carry inside. They hold on longer and longer with each dive they make, outdoing themselves until Don't Breathe In becomes as natural as Breathe In Breathe Out.

You sink or swim in this world. That's what my mother told me again and again.

~~~

"AND WHAT is hell? Can you tell me that?"
   "A pit full of fire."
   "And should you like to fall into that pit, and to be burning there for ever?"
   "No, sir."
   "What must you do to avoid it?"
   I deliberated a moment; my answer, when it did come, was objectionable:
"I must keep in good health, and not die."
   —Jane Eyre

THE GOLD freckles on her leather spine flickered in the streetlight that shone into my room. I held *Jane Eyre* close for our lost girl sleepover. One morning, I found a dent on my cheek from where her bound corner slept into me all night. I had a Jane Eyre tattoo of sorts, but it faded by the time I got to summer school. No one would see her story in my face. No one would believe it anyway.

I am going to introduce you to the number i, Mr. Martin said as we all walked into the library and sat down at the round table. The i refers to imaginary numbers, but don't get hung up on the word "imaginary." These numbers are no more or less imaginary than any other number. It's just that they can do things that real numbers can't do.

Mr. Martin went over to the reference section and took the dictionary from the shelf. He flipped through the pages until he found the word he was looking for. *So, the dictionary definition of the word "imagine" is to form a mental image.*

He came back to the table and sat down. He wiped the back of his neck with his washcloth and looked at us to see if we were following him. *Imaginary numbers just require a little more mental imaging, that's all,* he said.

You can do anything with numbers.

Examples of *imagine* in a sentence:
*I think there's someone in the house! Oh, you're just **imagining** things.*
*I can't **imagine** why you kept it a secret for so long.*

POETS CAN do whatever they want. I could go anywhere.
Decades after the Apollo 11 moon landing, Michael Collins is dubbed The Forgotten Astronaut. He is famous for being forgotten.

EVEN THOUGH I had failed algebra the first time, I understood the power of counting things. Some teachers counted to ten to hold it together. I counted things in plain sight that seemed forgotten or ignored—like a lopsided pink star made of paper and glitter that floated alone on a string in a third-floor apartment window. Whenever I walked by that apartment and looked up at that star, it seemed to come alive in front of my eyes and thank me and shine a shade pinker.

Michael Collins said he didn't feel lonely or abandoned circling to the dark side of the moon where no one could see him and no one could reach him. He said he found ways to feel connected to everyone else while floating alone.

I stood on a chair in the kitchen at two in the morning. *Keep it together,* I told myself as I stood taller than a body ever thought it could be. Such a difference a couple of feet made to my wide-awake thoughts. I looked outside the kitchen window from my new giant height and noticed a strand of silver Mardi Gras beads caught in the top branches of the crepe myrtle tree. I added it to my list of overlooked things. If Brahmagupta had kept such a list, it would have included zero.

Plants have bodies. I found this out when I picked out *The Secret Life of Plants* from the living room bookshelf and brought it to my room for a week or two. Plants move their bodies and communicate like any other living thing. The only reason we don't notice is because plants move like slow-motion dancers, and we move like rockets.

The apartment held its breath as I got ready to head out for another day in summer school. I couldn't stand to leave the place again and again looking so forgotten. *Hold it together,* I whispered to the living room. I brought the asparagus fern from the kitchen and put her on the table. I brought the African violet and the jade plant from the living room windowsill to join her. There were no thorns in our group. I named the fern George after reading about George Washington Carver in *The Secret Life of Plants.* George, Violet, and Jade sat in a semicircle on the table. I could feel them feel me as I ate my breakfast cereal. I could feel them thank me as I watered their small circles of soil. We weren't so alone clustered together in the middle with each other.

WHEN I started babysitting, my mother told me it was my turn now to buy my own clothes. Julie took me to a thrift store on Oak Street. We hunted through piles of old pants and found a few jeans that fit. We sewed peace symbol patches on the worn-out places.

Julie lived in a big house in the Garden District with two parents and three siblings and a dog named Coach and her own room with a double-sized waterbed. When I slept over at Julie's, I was a tourist in the foreign world of two parents with money. I was a tourist minding my manners and trying to blend in with the locals. Her mother would cook us dinner and let us eat in Julie's room, where she had her own stereo and a portable television. Her bedroom walls were painted chocolate brown with an off-white trim. Spending the night in her room was like sleeping in a slice of cake.

I brought my latest talisman from the living room bookshelf over to Julie's house for her to look through. She liked unusual things. *Be Here Now* by Ram Dass was kind of like the book about swamis that was written by the yogi, except the cover was purple and the writer was living. These random words were waiting inside when I skimmed through the pages—*unbearable compassion*, AUM, *the heart cave*. I read enough passages to get the gist of his words—that the past and the future can make our minds nervous. That here and now is the crest of a wave we can ride if try. I can't say it entirely made sense to me then, but I wanted it to.

We looked through Julie's records. Julie was the kind who liked rock and roll, and I was the kind who liked soul. We settled on B. B. King and his kind of blues.

It never occurred to me that it never occurred to her that I didn't know exactly where either of my parents was.

I had a swami mommie. She mastered the art of setting me aside. I don't think I was supposed to tell anyone. I don't think I ever did.

In the space between my thumb and my index finger, I wrote JANE in small red letters. On the other hand, I wrote SWAMI in small blue letters. The three of us went everywhere together, and I could feel them feeling me.

I sat on a bench on the Tulane campus. I read through my algebra workbook and pretended I was a student there. A student from a town up north where it snows in the winter and people wear turtleneck sweaters. A student with straight As in mathematics who came to study something hard and important at Tulane University. A student with a family who calls on the weekends and asks *How is everything going?* and *What did you do today?*

I picked different streets and biked to the very end of those streets. I sat on the levee and felt the river feeling me. I circumambulated Audubon Park and felt the secret lives of the cypress trees and the Spanish moss and the Saint Augustine grass. I sat on the fat roots of a live oak tree by the lagoon.

The trees knew me, knew all about me, and had seen worse. They were still there after hundreds of years of worse. They let me sit on their roots until I was ready to go—the way I let the fat black ants that lived on the tree crawl across my hands and legs until they found their way off. The bark on the oak trees looked like the hides of elephants. Their limbs looked like the trunks of elephants. Their tears looked like the summer rain running down their cheeks.

I walked to the Milton H. Latter Branch Library on Saint Charles Avenue between Dufossat and Soniat Streets. The library mansion was bought in 1948 by Milton's parents after he was killed in Okinawa during the Second World War. His parents wanted everyone to know him. They wanted everyone to be rich with Milton, so they turned their son into a mansion and turned the mansion into a library and gave it to everyone to make everyone better.

Every time I visited the Milton H. Latter Branch Library, I walked up and down the dramatic staircase with the wide wooden banister. I moved from room to rich room lined with books, thinking of Milton who came into the world and went away from the world and was so beloved he was still a part of the world, at least in the library where his name was stamped along the front edge of each book and engraved on the front of the two-story, neo-Italianate mansion. Couldn't everyone feel Milton in here?

I sat and listened to people talking about where they were going to eat lunch and how this summer was hotter than last summer and what direction that tropical storm off the coast of Florida was taking. No one could feel me listening to them.

Obituaries in the *Times-Picayune* always included the cause of death. We had a lot of gunshot causes and some knife wound causes, and of course cancer and stroke and car crash causes. I liked to look at the photos and think of each person who'd died and give them an extra goodbye. An old lady's face in the middle of the obits caught my eye. I can't remember her name, maybe a Juanita or a Marguerite. She had thick white hair and snappy black eyes and a happy micro-expression. I imagined she'd been my grandmother and had doted on me nonstop for fourteen years and even though she had died, I would be able to surf on the wave of her grandmotherliness for a lifetime.

I read her life story and the cause of her death. *She died from sadness and its complications.* My breath caught in my chest for a minute. On the second read, I saw that the sadness was really diabetes.

I could imagine exactly what it would have been like to be hugged by her. Her starched yellow housecoat with pressed creases, her chubby arms, the smell of hair spray and Ivory soap.

I watched the people on the campus and in the park and in the library the same way I watched Houdini in the late-night movie or Caine in the TV series *Kung Fu*. The Shaolin monk walked into a new town in the Wild West each week where he didn't know anyone, and he didn't say anything. He held it together. He watched from inside his heart cave.

I could watch like that for hours. I looked for what was overlooked while everyone else rocketed by.

The small and overlooked—

- the dime in the crack in the sidewalk on Freret and Calhoun
- the infinity sign I scratched into the side of the green light post a block away from school
- my initials on the underside of the library table
- the aqua-blue crystal marble I'd hidden on top of the shelf of the biography section in the school library
- the faded pink star in the apartment window
- and everything else in my home that summer

The big things we all shared—

- the moon
- everything on TV, especially the Watergate hearings, the weather report with three daily updates on any tropical storm lurking in the Gulf of Mexico, and the Indian head test pattern that stayed up all night at the end of regular programming
- *Jane Eyre*—all the other copies and editions that were in dozens of languages and thousands of libraries around the world
- the streetcars on Saint Charles Avenue
- and everything else outside of my home

Algebra comes from the Arabic word *al-jabr* and means "the reunion of broken parts."

Neil Armstrong took a giant step, but he said he felt very small. John Coltrane said he could start in the middle of a sentence and move in both directions at the same time.

KUNG FU reruns aired that summer on Thursday nights at 9 p.m. I could never get enough of the biracial boy named Kwai Chang Caine who had been abandoned by his parents and left in a Buddhist monastery somewhere in China. Unlike Jane, the teachers in his school loved him and taught him to build muscles in his empty places. The abandoned boy Caine grew into the kung fu man Caine. He could kick ass in black and white on our tiny Sony TV, and thousands of us set-asides would cheer him on every week.

After Caine passed all the kung fu tests in the Shaolin monastery, a dragon was tattooed on the insides of his forearms. The twin dragons of fate and courage would live with him forever. I tried to draw a dragon on my left forearm, but it looked like a rabbit. I washed it off and drew the number eight instead. When I straightened my arm, the eight stretched out as infinity. I drew another infinity on my right arm and fell asleep.

I ate sandwiches with cheddar cheese, lettuce, and honey. I ate cereal. The white bowl was a moon and the Cheerios her little moons.

Mr. Martin was out sick one day. The substitute didn't know any algebra, so he put us in teams of two and quizzed us instead on vocabulary. I won points for *pachyderm*—elephants are my favorite mammals. None of us could win the word *behoove*, even when used in sample sentences.

It would behoove me to look elsewhere for help.
Most of all it behooves us to take better care of one another.

Whenever Maggie's father dropped me off after babysitting, he waited in his tan station wagon until I got upstairs and turned on the porch light. That was our signal that I was in the apartment safe and sound. It never occurred to me that it never occurred to him that I was living alone that month and a half.

Teenagers love being on their own.

My mother had given me a large windup alarm clock earlier in the school year—a reward for doing a good job of waking her up every morning in time for her job. The clock was lemon yellow with a blue face and two silver bells on top. At first I thought it was a kind of a gag gift, but not as funny as a snakes-in-a-can kind of gag gift. If she'd asked me, I would have told her I wanted the *B. B. King in London* album. I would have played B. B. for her every morning to wake her up—*Caldonia, Caldonia. What makes your big head so hard?* Instead, I turned the television and the radio and all the noisy news all the way up to get her up and out of the bed.

Every night, I called TIME and listened to the woman with no accent say very calmly—*At the tone, the time will be . . .*

Now, now, now.

Pretty soon I couldn't sleep unless I had the loud ticking alarm clock close by. The sound relaxed me, like rain on the roof. My mother teased me that I was like a Saint Bernard puppy. For years, I thought she meant that I was able to rouse her from her fugue state each morning the way Saint Bernard dogs are able to rescue hypothermic hikers lost in the Alps or find tourists snowed under by an avalanche. Turns out the Saint Bernard part was incidental—some dog owners wrap a ticking clock in an old towel hoping the crying puppy will be fooled into thinking the sound is their mother's heartbeat. For some puppies, a disembodied fake heart wrapped in a rag was better than nothing.

In our heart cave, where we are now, we watch the entire drama that is our lives. We watch the illusion with unbearable compassion.—Ram Dass

〜

I CUT summer school to bike to Lake Pontchartrain with Julie. She brought two tabs of windowpane acid for our day trip to the lake.

Counting helped, biking helped, getting high helped, Lake Pontchartrain helped.

We sat on the seawall where cement steps led right down into the salty lake. The sky was clear, and the air felt lighter than usual. We looked out over the lake whose other side was too far to spot. Blue was the only thing we could see as far as we could see—as though we were sitting inside a blue crystal marble.

We didn't say anything for a long while. I thought I was hallucinating the tiny threads that floated in the air above us from somewhere across the lake. I could see a smattering of threads catch on a branch in the tree beside us and one in Julie's hair and a couple on the spokes of our bicycle wheels.

And then I saw a tiny baby spider on one of the silky threads that landed on me. I could feel it feeling me with eight tiny legs on the sun-bleached hair of my right arm.

When I turned around, there were dozens of threads in the air, barely visible, on the benches and bushes, on the antennas of the cars that drove by. It was like an invisible ticker-tape parade and the spiders were welcoming us home.

You are completely safe, I whispered to the spider on my arm.
We are completely infinite, I imagined from the spider.

Spider hatchlings can move through the air by releasing one or more gossamer threads to catch the wind. They've been known to survive without food while traveling in air currents of jet streams for twenty-five days or longer.

Who are you talking to? Julie asked.

I showed her the speck of a spider. Then I showed her all the other threads floating around us.

Scores of people walked by with dogs, with Frisbees, with kids in strollers. No one else noticed the new arrivals descending.

Do you think it's real? Julie asked.

The Romans didn't see zero for centuries after it was discovered in India, but it was still real. We lay down in the grass and watched the silk threads against the blue sky.

I would have to revise my list of things only I saw. Who knew how many tiny beings I never noticed saw the same things I saw with their miniature eyes?

After the flurry of spiders had landed, we got back on our bikes for the long ride back home. We stood on an overpass and watched the flurry of midday traffic fly underneath without noticing us noticing them.

George Washington Carver believed that when a living thing is loved enough, it will reveal itself to us. Was it the spider that had been revealed to me or the other way around?

This is a story I revealed to myself.

~~~

YEARS LATER, Julie leaves the earth first. She dies young in her late thirties from a liver worn out and wrung out from drugging and drinking. Most of our friends do the same kind of leaving one way or another before they're forty-five. A few go missing and never come back, but I keep on surviving each year out of habit. Like Michael Collins said—Put LUCKY on my tombstone.

~~~

OUTSIDE WAS everywhere I could go that my mother was not—the Crescent City, the Gulf of Mexico, the new moon in the full black sea of sky looking for her in its circular way and coming up empty, only a thumbnail of light.

On an episode of *Marcus Welby, M.D.*, a runaway boy cut school and rode alone up and down the hills of San Francisco in a trolley car. The trolley car driver grew concerned for the teen and gave him a sandwich and drove him back home to his family.

In New Orleans, there is a place for a passenger to stand at the front of the streetcar next to the driver. There's a rail to hold onto and a big front window to look out from. I rode streetcars when I couldn't sleep and sometimes in the afternoons. The bumpy ride, the wooden benches, the pale-yellow light, the windows open to catch a muggy breeze, the squeal of the air brakes as we came to a stop to let someone on, let someone off—a ritual for my solo hours so I could only be where I was.

Late is okay, but you can never be early, the driver explained to me one afternoon. He slowed the streetcar to a crawl. *People count on the schedule to get to work. If you're on time or late, they'll be able to catch you. But if you're early, you'll end up leaving without them.*

The streetcar driver's name was Gifford. He drove mostly at night from uptown to downtown and back again in a circle. I could go anywhere.

We swayed down Saint Charles Avenue like we were riding an Indian elephant at the end of a long day. I liked it best this way, when we moved slow, like thunder.

Never go faster than your slowest member. A safety tip in a guidebook for hikers.

I would wait on the sidewalk and watch the streetcars as they passed until I saw Gifford at the front of one. He let me get on without a fare and I'd stand next to him. I'd ride his streetcar just to hear him ask me—*How was your day?* and *How are you doing?*

Gifford had been to Vietnam. He showed me his beat-up feet and told me about walking in wet boots through miles of rice fields for weeks on end. He showed me a photo of himself sitting on a stool, peeling a mountain of potatoes. He was shaved and shorn in the photo—no Afro, no mustache, no soul patch and sideburns. He told me about little kids in Vietnam with nothing to eat and how he gave them candy bars that he carried around. He didn't tell me about the rest of the war.

It was the summer of secrets and imaginary numbers.

Apollo was a silver swami poised in the endless sky.

～～

AT THE foot of my bed was a stuffed monkey I'd named Mimi. She had a baby on her back. When you turned the baby clockwise, a lullaby would tinkle from somewhere inside of Mimi, who never woke up no matter what while her baby spun in circles counter-clockwise above her.

Gifford invited me to meet him in Audubon Park on a Saturday afternoon. This wasn't a date. This is just what I did with my friends on the weekends. We met in the front of the park by the fountain with the statue of a woman dancing on water. She was naked except for the scarves wrapped around her. I counted nine pennies underwater waiting to come true. Gifford told me I was his good luck. We walked to the Mushroom, and I bought the new *Temptations Anthology* three-LP set with money I'd saved from babysitting. Gifford picked out a ring made from the handle of a silver teaspoon and bought it for me.

It didn't seem strange to me that I was so young and he was all grown. Just like it didn't seem strange that I was so young and left on my own. I'd just been skipped ahead a few grades with so much to learn.

Gifford gave me his telephone number. I memorized it. I didn't think I would use it, but I liked having his number inside my mind.

Campgrounds don't have phone numbers. My mother had my name underneath her, and everywhere she went, I was there.

George Washington Carver wanted to know the name of every stone, plant, insect, and animal. He wanted to know how each got their colors. He wanted to know their purpose, their reason for being, but there was no one to answer his questions. He said he asked anyway. He said he asked the flowers.

Part 3

The domain of the imagination is reality.

—GUILLAUME APOLLINAIRE

SOMETIMES THAT SUMMER, I went into my mother's closet and looked around at her clothes still there. Sometimes I wore one of her brand-new shirts because I liked new clothes, and she wasn't home. My favorite was a tight-fitting cotton-weave shirt the color of the desert with thin strips of pale blue embedded in the sand like rare streams of water. I liked to wear it even just around the house. I liked to turn all the way around in my mother's closet and let my cheek brush against the crowd of rayon, silk, and cotton shoulders.

I didn't go in looking for it, but I knew somewhere in between all the shoulders hung my worry—*Will she come back?*

It's the yogi she'll come home for. Not Jane and all her trouble.

I knew the way her tiny silver Honda Z shook each time a truck passed her on the highway. I knew her plans were up in the air, just two freelancers and a whole lot of road.

I knew she nursed another plan to drive up to Alaska before the pipeline was built. She had talked about taking me out of school for a year and driving the 4,367 miles to Anchorage. How we might have to stop along the way and get waitressing jobs for a few months now and then when we ran out of money. I was brave for Alaska—as long as I was in the car sitting beside her.

Before human beings traveled to outer space and took pictures of our planet, philosophers and photographers and travelers predicted that we would take much better care of each other once we could see Earth from a distance. Once we could travel away and look back at our small, exposed selves.

My mother's Dr. Scholl's sandals lay on the floor of her closet. Well-worn brown footprints shined from the insoles as though she had just stepped out of the shower and left two wet prints there. As though they'd turned to fossils a thousand years ago. Either way, I found her any way I could.

I didn't feel psychic, but when I put on the desert T-shirt, I could feel New Mexico all around me. I could see her camping, the stars over her head, complementing her.

If my mother left the planet and didn't come back, would I feel the moment her secret life left? Would her three plants on the dining room table feel it along with me? Would the police come and knock on my door and take me somewhere? What would happen to me then? I circled August 1 on the kitchen calendar. Surely, she'd be home by the time August arrived.

Possibilities for a Plan B

> —Julie's house for a couple of nights
>
> —Julie's friend Buddy, who was a Vietnam vet and didn't like living alone
>
> —The fourplex's shed for a couple of nights
>
> —Gifford might give me some money

My father was an *x* living in Bakersfield, California. He told me he was too far removed to be a real part of my life.

My father had a sister he didn't like very much and didn't speak to at all. She lived in Washington, DC, and I met her a few times. I definitely liked her and so did my mom. She was tall and dramatic like Katharine Hepburn, except her accent was southern. She didn't have any kids. She drank too much and one time she drank rubbing alcohol and had to be hospitalized. She invented stories to tell me at night when I was in grade school and she'd come for a visit. She showed me how to rub my eyes long enough so I'd see shooting stars in the dark space of my room when she turned off the light.

A framed poster of Earth from the moon's surface hung on the wall of the library at school. Sometimes Mr. Martin used the poster to make the point that the power of numbers got us to the moon and back. Sometimes I used the poster to see how close together we are even when we are not.

Magnificent desolation—what Buzz Aldrin said when first seeing Earth from the surface of the moon.

⁓

ON THE weekends, before the day got too thick and too hot, before the swelling cumulonimbus clouds took over the sky and broke apart like an afternoon war, I would bike over to the front of Audubon Park. I'd sit on a bench and watch the bright topsail of a cloud grow into view over the treetops.

You can find something good in the shape of some trees—the sun on their crown, their arms lifting up, twirling like a dancer shimmering in green.

When you need to seal in a good feeling, like air in your lungs before making a deep dive, it helps to say a meaningful word to yourself while looking up at the crown of a good tree. A word like AUM, like *uplifting*, a word like *infinity* or *swami*. All of this will seem strange at first, until you need to do it.

Ram Dass could do it. He said he practiced *turning trees into people*. I think he meant he practiced this when he was lonely. I turned loneliness into trees and trees into dancers.

Sometimes a tourist, looking for the zoo, would get off of the streetcar at the park's front entrance. On one side of the entrance was a stone sign that read PARK. On the other side of the entrance was a stone sign that read ZOO. But there was no zoo in sight. The tourist would look around and find only the absence of zoo. A zero zoo and no directions for how to solve for zoo.

Sometimes the tourist would ask me for help because I looked friendly when I sat on a bench immeasurably uplifted. Sometimes they were from another country and would use a few words of English—*zoo, where, bus*—mixed in with their language, French, Swahili, Korean. And I would use a few words of English—*one mile, hot, walk*—and point out the way. I would make sure they drank some water from the fountain before they started walking. Most times I would get on my bike and see if they had made it.

Sometimes I would run into Peanut Butter Man. Word was he had dodged the draft by mixing Quaaludes with peanut butter and eating that every day until he lost his mind and his hair turned gray. All he did was ride around the park on his bicycle looking for women walking alone. At first you don't notice the tip of his dick that poked out from the bottom of his short cutoff jeans. Then you do and you feel embarrassed for him until you compare notes with any other girl who ever walked alone in the park. It made you wonder. Then you stop wondering. And you carry a whistle and you keep your eyes open. You understand all too well that you live in a world full of Peanut Butter Men and women with whistles.

~~

MAGGIE NEEDED a babysitter on the Fourth of July. She took my hand and showed me her bears and lions and kittens and penguins.

She's scared of fireworks, her older brother Todd told me as he put on his tennis shoes. *She has a lot of fear.*

No, I don't! said Maggie. *I have a lot of stuffed animals.*
Same thing, said Todd.

Master Po on *Kung Fu* was always teaching Caine the real meaning of strength. He told him that the obvious ways to be strong are rarely the best ways.

The original meaning of *kung fu* was not simply the practice of a Chinese martial art. Kung fu refers to excellence achieved through long practice in any endeavor. In the colloquial, one can say that a person's kung fu is Creole cooking and someone else's kung fu might be semicursive calligraphy.

Mr. Martin's kung fu was algebra and civics.
Jane Eyre's kung fu was her resilient heart cave.
My mother's kung fu was in flying away without missing anyone.
I wanted to achieve her kind of excellence.

I wrote KUNG on the sole of my left foot in red ink and FU on the sole of my right foot in blue ink. I put on my huarache sandals and walked the long sweaty mile to summer school.

Part 4

Strength—the capacity to withstand
great force or pressure.

IT WAS A THURSDAY NIGHT and *Kung Fu* had just ended. Caine
had been sparring the way Shaolin monks do. One of the other
students had beaten his sparring partners with a show of aggres-
sion that draws a crowd. Caine was in awe of the monk's strength,
but his teacher was not. He told young Caine that violence has no
mind.

Jane Eyre was open on my bed. Jane had just walked out of Thorn-
field Hall and onto the moors. Even the moors can look beautiful.
Even Mr. Rochester would lose sight of her.

There was some money in the envelope my mother left in the
kitchen drawer for groceries and the occasional cheeseburger. It
was 10 p.m. and I could go anywhere. There was a chance the
K&B on Saint Charles Avenue and Broadway would still be making
cheeseburgers.

I hadn't done much of anything the day before, July Fourth, except
babysit for Maggie. Summer school had closed for the holiday, and
Mr. Martin and the other summer school students and Maggie's
family and my mother and her boyfriend and everyone had been
somewhere looking at fireworks, spread out on blankets, with dogs

and kids running around, music playing, and Julie out of town. A mile walk to the K&B on the day after the Fourth for a cheeseburger and cola seemed like a small thing I could do.

～～

SAINT CHARLES Avenue was the most famous avenue in all of New Orleans, with streetcars traveling back and forth on the grassy neutral ground and where rich people you never saw showed off houses that looked like sugar. I felt I was safe on Saint Charles, even if the sidewalks were dark with tree shadows.

But a forest-green pickup truck circled around several times—into the neutral ground, across the streetcar tracks, and back around to pass me on the sidewalk again—his red hair, red neck, him looking at me.

I crossed the avenue once or twice to lose him the way I'd lost other men on other days. I thought it had worked until there was the man outside his truck, standing on the dark sidewalk not far from me. He asked me for directions to the fireworks at Lake Pontchartrain since he was from out of town. It was the fifth of July, and the fireworks were over, and I didn't know the directions anyway. I turned to walk away, and he grabbed my arm. I was one block away from the K&B on the corner.

I saw the knife in his hand down by his side. I froze the way an animal might freeze right before being killed. He said, *If you move or scream you are a fucking dead duck.*

The way *fuck* and *duck* rhymed. He pulled me closer to the knife aimed at my guts. The way my guts made a fist.

The world split open and wobbled. The way I was sure someone driving by could see this and stop this. The way no one could see this knife by his side. He promised he'd kill me if I made any sound as we walked arm in arm to the narrow side street and his truck parked in the dark.

The way I should have jumped out of his truck while he was driving away. But who would help me after I jumped? He'd get to me first and kill me right then. The way I wanted to Not die Not die Not die and felt like I was dying.

The way I calculated how many days from Thursday it would take before someone would miss me. Maybe by the middle of next week, after enough summer school absences, five days away. But no one would be home to get a call from the school office.

He wanted to drive to the lake or maybe across it to Mississippi. What were the chances he would bring me back here? He said he hadn't decided if he'd kill me or not. The way I bargained and he unzipped his pants and made me touch his pink dick. The way I persuaded him to stay uptown and rape me in the park. That way, if I got away, I was still close to home. That way, if I didn't and he dumped me dead in the lagoon, someone I knew might ID me the next day. Then when my mother came back, she'd know I hadn't just run away. And I, as a dead girl, wouldn't feel so all alone in the endless dark sky.

The way I heard someone walk by as I took off my clothes inside the dark truck. Who walks in this park so late at night? Who would believe this was a rape taking place? The way this rape could get worse if I shouted right now. I turned very small. He still had a knife, and the footsteps went away, and my silence stayed with me, and he thanked me right then for being on *his side*.

The way my arms kept pushing him away without thinking. The way I cried, and he said—*Do I have to tie you up?* The way I said *No.* He took over my body while I waited on the moon. The way I floated for hours on the dark side of pain. You sink or swim in this world.

The way I sank. The way I swam.

You were no virgin, he said after. *There's no way you are just fourteen years old.*

39

I nodded, because that's what you do when you've been raped by someone who still might drive off to Mississippi with you in their truck. Someone who still hasn't decided if he's going to kill you or not. Someone who needs to believe that this was no rape, that you are not fourteen, that there's no way you're a virgin.

We drove around the park while he pretended we'd been out on a date. I nodded, because that's what you do when a date with a rapist is better than a trip to Mississippi with one. The way I thanked him for the date.

He kept driving around the park and uptown and past Tulane and Loyola and back to the park, pretending and deciding.

Tell me if you're going to call the cops so I can be ready, you know, to get out of town sooner.

I wouldn't I wouldn't I wouldn't. Why would I? The way the policemen would want to reach my unreachable mother. The way we miss our only worlds if they're taken away. The way Alan Shepard cried when he stood on the moon and looked back at Earth in 1971.

It's a nice night. I'll walk.

The way he let me open the truck's door at the next corner and go. He asked for my name, and I gave him someone else's.

The way I ran a kind of limping, hobbled run the six blocks home. I left my shoes and underwear on the floor of his truck. Two men on the sidewalk shouted something at me. The way I hated them. I looked back to see if they were chasing me, if the truck was circling around for me. The way pain shot through me as I ran, and blood dripped down my legs and soaked the crotch of my pants. The way I bled for three days.

This happened on a Thursday, the day named for Thor.

Thursday was the night I first piled three silver pots and some glass ashtrays in front of the door, like Laura Petrie did on the *Dick Van Dyke Show*. I began my practice of laying my head where my feet used to go, so I could see through the living room to the big front door with the too-little lock and my homemade alarm. That way I could sleep until it came crashing down.

This is the story of thunder.

Part 5

Endow the Living with the Tears
You squander on the Dead.

—EMILY DICKINSON

THERE'S A TINY SPECK at the corner of the eyelid near the bridge of the nose and it's called a punctum. When I was in grade school, I held an onion near my face while I looked in the mirror and pulled down my eyelid. I waited for my tiny speck to produce a stream of onion tears. Turns out that tears do not come from this miniature orifice. Instead, the punctum is a drain for tears that naturally fill our eyes all through the day. When we cry, the small drain becomes overwhelmed. Our eyes are not suited for a flood of sad feelings.

I forgot to bring my washcloth. I forgot to bring my book. I sat in the school library surrounded by numbers and books and felt the feeling of nothing, like the space inside zero that holds everything together. I put my head on the wooden table and listened to Mr. Martin go on about numbers. He drew a large oval on the green board and in it he wrote RATIONAL NUMBERS. Then he drew another oval next to the rational one and wrote IRRATIONAL NUMBERS. I didn't think about numbers. I thought about the ovals Mrs. Harrigan had drawn on the green board during health class last year. Inside the space of the ovals she'd written the word *impregnated*. Then she lectured us on the importance of guarding our eggs at all costs.

Please let me be not impregnated. I prayed to all the infinite numbers in the universe. I prayed to the one moon and the many moors, to the top of the trees and the lagoon in the park and to the school that I sat in full of summer school teachers. I covered every space I could see with my one single prayer. *Please let me be not impregnated.*

I stayed after class and helped Mr. Martin sort through his papers. Wouldn't he see the things my face had to say? Then maybe he'd bring me to his house where I would babysit his son and help out his wife. She might comb my hair and make me a sandwich and let me sleep on their couch where it would feel so much safer. They would hear my telling and keep my secrets. And I'd go back home in August when my mother returned.

I hinted. I talked about the recent case of a teacher in another school who had been raped in the parking lot by a man she carpooled with.

That kind of happened to me, I said. *Last night.*
I held my breath like a diver.
Mr. Martin didn't look up from his papers. He reached for his briefcase and put his notebooks inside.
Men can't understand rape, he said.

I turned to go. I walked over to the biography shelf to look at the aqua-blue crystal marble I'd hidden there. I could see a tiny row of library windows reflected on the surface of the small planet. I could see myself barely there. Everything was in miniature— upside down, reversed, and better.

I am alone now, truly alone, and absolutely isolated . . . I am it.—Michael Collins

～～

WHEN I got home from school, I put the Thursday clothes in a paper bag and took them to the trash can in the parking lot behind the apartment building. They'd have to wait there until the trash was picked up on Monday. But when I got back upstairs, I could still hear them crying. After an hour, I brought the clothes inside. I washed them by hand and then hid them under a box at the back of my closet. It was the best I could do. They quieted down or else they just died.

~~~

MAGGIE NEEDED a babysitter Saturday night. Her mother called me. *Are you free?*

Was I free? I was numb and I was nothing. I said yes.

If you can find nothing, then is it nothing or is it something?

She's already asleep, Maggie's mother said. *She probably won't wake up at all and will never even know we were gone, but here's a number where you can reach me. Eat anything you want in the fridge.*

I didn't eat anything. I sat different on the same couch I'd sat on the day before Thursday. I sat barely there. I counted the flowers I found in the florid couch fabric and the embroidered footstool. Then Maggie woke up.
They didn't tell me they were going away!
I picked her up. She held on tight and cried into my neck. Our cheeks pressed next to each other, and our dark waves of hair fell together like drapes.
You're completely safe, I told her. *No one's going to hurt you.*
Tears overwhelmed my eyes and mingled with hers where our cheeks pressed together. I rubbed her back in circles as we held onto each other. She circled my hair around her small fingers.

There's a ghost in my room, Maggie said when she stopped crying.
She stood in the doorway of her room and directed me to the animals in need of rescuing. In her house, I was the hero.

In my house, I was the hero, the ghost, and the one in trouble.

I brought Maggie into the living room.
I can stay here with you? she asked. *I won't get in trouble?*

Who wants to stay in a room with a ghost? I said.

I tell my animals all my secrets.

I tell the plants, I said. *You can tell plants anything. They have hundreds of ears and they can hear everything.*

Do they have eyes? Maggie asked.

I don't think they have eyes, I said. *But they don't need eyes, because they can feel what you look like and they can feel what you're feeling.*

According to legend, the great Bodhisattva Chenrezig made a vow that he would not rest until he'd freed all living things from all kinds of suffering, like an inmate trying to break everyone out of San Quentin penitentiary. Like the greatest escape artist trick ever. After a while, Chenrezig looked around at the huge number of inmates still locked up in pain. He freaked out. His head blew up into thousands of pieces. Amitabha Buddha pulled Chenrezig back together, but this time with a body better suited for his vow—with eleven heads and a thousand arms fanned out around him, feeling everyone feeling everything.

Emotional tears have a viscosity and structure that set them apart from lubricant tears or irritant tears. And each type of emotion creates its own molecular landscape. Sorrow's tears look like an aerial photo after a tornado has blown out half of the town. The high school is gone. All you can see are the foundations and angles where homes used to stand and well-traveled streets are now broken in half. But the tears full of laughter have swimming pools in back yards and parks full of swings—the town before the tornado arrived.

My tears are like towns where a twister has been spotted. A siren is blaring and no one feels safe.

Do I have to tie you up?

～～

MAGGIE SAT next to me on the couch with her feet tucked under. She pulled her arms inside her yellow pajama top and hugged herself in the air-conditioned room. Seven frightened bears and

46

kittens sat with us. Seven pairs of unblinking eyes and seven pairs of alert fuzzy ears.

Do you believe in ghosts? she asked me.

I guess so. They're like negative numbers. They show you what's gone missing.

I pulled the crocheted afghan from the back of the couch and covered Maggie. *If you want to trick a ghost, just stare at something for a long time. Soon that's all you can see, and no ghost can drag you into the past with them. Also, counting helps.*

Maggie and I stared at the peace lily on top of the television set. We chose the lily's single white bloom for our focus. We decided to count slowly to 101. We made it to the forties before Maggie fell asleep leaning against me, holding a traumatized brown bear.

Trauma gives rise to complicated, sometimes uncanny alterations of consciousness, which George Orwell, one of the committed truth-tellers of our century, called "doublethink," and which mental health professionals . . . call "dissociation."—Judith Lewis Herman, *Trauma and Recovery*

～～

IF YOU grow up in New Orleans, you are Catholic by osmosis. You are catholic in your *eclectic* knowledge of things like holy days. Like how the right knee is reserved for divine adoration where genuflecting is concerned. You know all manner of saints—the athletes and the ascetics, the popular and the obscure. Half the streets bear their names, and half the schools are Our Ladys.

Our Lady of the Lake
Our Lady of Prompt Succor
Visitation of Our Lady

You've crossed over Annunciation on a regular basis without thinking twice to get to the river. Jesus of Loyola is one of your neighbors. You've grown up seeing him on his lawn all hours of the day and night, baring his naked heart as he stares at the drama unfolding before him on Saint Charles Avenue. He has to stand there and take it all. It's enough to make you cry.

And of course, there are the thousands of Our Ladys in miniature all over town in front yards of all kinds. You grow up thinking every city is this full of saints until you move out of state where the street names strike you as stunningly uninspired.

~~~

MR. MARTIN pointed to the number line that was still on the green board. *What if there were numbers that held the answers to questions and problems, but they weren't on the number line?* He looked at us for a response and we looked back without one. *And what if you could put on a jet pack and fly, not just east and west with these numbers, but up and over? Well, that's how you find the world of imaginary numbers.*

Mr. Martin had us come up to the board and write little *i*'s in the green sky above the number line highway because that's how a civics teacher teaches algebra in summer school.

If I could name buildings:

Our Lady Promptly Swims across the Lake to Help Whenever You Need Her
Immaculate Cave of Unbearable Compassion
Our Lady of Sacred Zero Which Can Never Be Broken

Mr. Martin wiped the chalk from his hands and sat down in the circle. *When the numbers we had didn't solve the problems at hand, people found new numbers. We did* NOT *invent them. They were always there, like zero, waiting for us to find them and the answers that they held. Still, it took ages for the world to notice zero.*

What you see is what you get.

~~~

AT NIGHT, my ears were two bloodhounds without a leash following every sound. There was a faint clicking that took me a week to locate. I'd looked everywhere for its source. I even timed the intervals between the clicks—twenty seconds, six seconds, twelve seconds. The pattern repeated, but I couldn't break the code. Then as I headed out to summer school one morning and waited for the light on the corner to change, a clunking sound hung above me and I looked up. Twenty seconds of green, six seconds of yellow, and twelve seconds of red.

In the Thai solar calendar, Thursday is associated with the color orange.
In Australia, most workers are paid on Thursday.
In astrology, Thursday is associated with Sagittarius and Jupiter, the planet of abundance and good luck.

On just one planet, there are so many Thursday worlds all swimming together in the very same pool on the very same day. I wanted an orange Thursday. Not a Thursday associated with an abundance of shame.

The way he pretended it was a date while I agreed and stayed small.

We all want to escape death.—Houdini

I wanted to forget Thursday. I wanted to move as far from thunder as I possibly could.

Thor's Day's child has far to go.

I brought the Random House dictionary into my room. I wondered if other people picked words at random from dictionaries and books to help them find answers they couldn't find elsewhere.

Later, I will learn it's a thing with a name—*bibliomancy* is a practice that uses books for divination, for *magical medicine,* for removing negativities, for providing insightful answers to unanswered questions. This is the way I wasn't all alone all the time.

Jane Eyre turned to books when there was no one left to trust.

I let the pages of the large dictionary flip-flop back and forth between my palms. I wanted a word just for me in that moment. The pages fell open in the *As*. I closed my eyes and let my finger land on a word.

ag·gra·vat·ed ˈa-grə-ˌvā-təd
adjective

an offense made worse, as in the use of a deadly weapon [kidnapping, rape]

I couldn't let that word stay in my room overnight. Some words that show up are not talismans at all. Instead, they push their way forward like a bad dream with a fever.

I concentrated harder for better word medicine waiting for me like imaginary numbers waited up and over the normal number line. I flipped the heavy pages back and forth again. This time the dictionary fell open in the *Ss* and my finger landed on

spell ˈspel
noun

a spoken word or form of words held to have magic power

~~~~

I WAS sitting in algebra class when the blood came.

Mr. Martin was in the middle of reading a quote about algebra being metaphysical. The flock of *i*'s we'd drawn was still flying above the east-west highway. I asked Mr. Martin for a pass to the girl's restroom.

Dear Our Lady of the Blessed Menstruation,
    Thank God I'm not pregnant.

Mr. Martin had no idea what a horror the girls' restroom was—how not a single toilet worked, ever. How the toilets were chronically stopped up with bloody Kotex and shit. How during the regular school year, the girls' bathroom was just a place to buy dope, write graffiti, smoke, fight, or fuck. I felt like I might vomit.

During summer school the bathroom was mostly empty. I jammed my washcloth into my underpants and headed home. For each block on the long sweaty walk, I counted how many humid breaths I inhaled and exhaled. Counting this way kept me from fainting. Numbers can do anything.

The cramps were furious—as though my uterus was slicing its own lining to shreds first before spitting it out. As though the lining were the underpants I left in the truck on Thursday, July 5. As though my pelvis was finally able to scream and kick and punch the closest thing it could find.

I took it all. It was enough to make me cry. It was enough to make me vomit right there on the curb. I threw up happy and I threw up angry and I threw up hoping to turn myself inside out and start all over.

~~~

IN 1975, Loyola University opened a women's center in a small shotgun house on the outskirts of campus. They offered workshops for women in basic auto repair and financial planning. They also taught classes in assertiveness training.

Learn to—

- *speak up, make requests, ask why*
- *question authority*
- *and make things better for yourself*

Join our next class. Four weeks, just $20.

Maybe a college senior would lead the class and have us sit in a circle in the new women's center with posters of Angela Davis and Gloria Steinem on the walls and a round shag rug on the floor. A striped spider plant might hang in the window, heavy with clutches of baby spider plants. Maybe we would role-play things getting better for ourselves and for others. We'd learn how to speak up, name our secrets, and question authority, as in—*Where were you when your authority was needed?* We'd turn ourselves inside out and start over together.

Twenty bucks was never easy to come by.

This is a kind of do-it-yourself love story.

America—Love It or Leave It: a bumper sticker, 1970s.

Vietnam—Love It or Leave It: another bumper sticker, 1970s.

Later in college, I asked a professor—*If you don't know what you never had, if you just learned not to feel it, how can you then ask for it assertively?* She said something about how we unknowingly find ways to fill in the gaps.

The mathematician Muḥammad ibn Mūsā al-Khwārizmī wrote the first book about algebra in Baghdad around AD 825. The title has been translated to mean *The Book of Restoration and Balancing*.

~~

I LIKED it best when I hung out with Gifford and Julie and our other friends at the front of Audubon Park—our feet in the fountain, trying to cool down on another hot day. Gifford knew what had happened to me, but I never told Julie. I felt like I'd failed after being skipped ahead a grade and into her class.

We'd sit in a circle at the park and share a quart of Dixie Beer and a couple of joints, and I would look for things no one else saw. The numbers embossed on the bottom of the beer bottle, the freckle of jet high above us with a cabin full of travelers unable to see me, the chameleon in the grass by the bench who, for the time being, was a shade of pale green. Instead of a long lizard tail tapering down to a thin gray whisk, there was just a short stump with a reddish nub and what looked like new growth, all pink, inside of the nub.

Lizards have developed a defense mechanism called *autonomy* whereby they drop or lose their tail when threatened by a predator.

Although the tail will regenerate over time, it will never be as long as it originally was, and the loss will affect the lizard's balance forever. The regeneration process can result in the lizard becoming nutritionally depleted.

Harry Houdini said that his audience never saw the hours of torturous self-training it took to overcome fear and master the illusion. They saw only the miraculous way he held it together.

I could see the lizard's tiny ribcage move with each tiny breath. By comparison, my breaths were as slow and deep as those of a gray whale. But we both breathed the air. We both had been held captive in the very same park and escaped with our lives.

Every escape exacts its own price. Both of us were regenerating and restoring some sort of balance. We were hiding in green in between living beings, and we'd never be as large as before.

It never occurred to me that it should have occurred to my mother to do more to protect me. What you get is what you get.

~~

ACCORDING TO pattern theory, we use the closest thing we can find, usually our hopes and understanding of the patterns around us, to fill in the gaps of what we don't know. In 1970, the psychophysical experiments of Warren and Warren illustrated how subjects did not perceive the sound that was missing.

Actual sound	Perceived words
the eel is on the shoe	the heel is on the shoe
the eel is on the car	the wheel is on the car
the eel is on the table	the meal is on the table

The actual sound did not reach consciousness, even though it's possible there could be an eel on a shoe or an eel on a car or an eel on a table about to be eaten. But the words that consciousness heard were the words most likely to exist, based on what we have come to expect or hope to find.

How I filled in the gaps around me:

Actual	Perceived
my mother is missing	my mother is missing me

What reached my consciousness, based on what I had come to expect, was that my mother needed me—to fend for myself, to fend for her, to hold down the fort, to hold things together, to swim and not sink. This is the way I knew I was good.

Part 6

When we contemplate the whole globe as one
great dewdrop, striped and dotted with continents
and islands, flying through space with other stars
all singing and shining together as one, the whole
universe appears as an infinite storm of beauty.

—JOHN MUIR, *TRAVELS IN ALASKA*

IN COLLEGE, in Ohio, none of the streets were saintly or French. None of the food was creole or special. Nothing at all was New Orleans anymore. I was way out of place. On the other hand, I found a few streets and a small-town motel named for Tecumseh. He was born in a village a few miles away. There was a rumor he'd been buried in one of the old earthen mounds on the grounds of our campus. No one was certain, but I knew that the connection I created out of thin air between Tecumseh and me was a home on the planet I carried around.

Right before graduation, I went home for a visit. My friends were all moving back to their hometowns, ready to deploy their new baccalaureates.

Other cities are better, my mother said. Meaning—don't move back here.

I went out into her small yard. I picked up the shears and returned to the chore of the day—pruning the ravenous wisteria that had refused to bloom even once in her yard. The wisteria had taken over the side of the arbor, loosened a beam, and threatened to pull down the whole thing while still reaching higher. My mother wanted the vine brought to heel.

She came outside with her cigarette and glass of white wine. The silver in her black hair sparkled in the sun. My mother was a head shorter than me, but she always stood tall with her good dancer's posture, her neck so regal, her collarbones proud. I climbed the ladder with the shears in one hand and half disappeared into the wild vine.

She wasn't the kind of person to need other people. That's what my mother told me once when I was alone in Ireland at eighteen years old. I was ready to come back after three months on an independent study project for college. I didn't use the word *lonely*, but my mother could sniff out my soft sides like a German shepherd sniffs out a bomb. I only ever told her I missed her one time after I'd moved out. She howled in complaint. *How can you miss me? You keep coming back.*

My mother gave me a set of framed black-and-white photos of myself from when I was three or four. There I was grinning for the camera as I pedaled my trike. And sitting in a rocking chair in my favorite striped pajamas. And small on the couch pretending to talk into the large telephone receiver. She wanted me back. She wanted me gone.

I cut the wisteria down to the ground. After I graduated from college, I moved to New York City. So Big and So Fast. I uprooted my fear and never moved back to my home below sea level.

~~~

I WORKED with heroin addicts in a methadone clinic on Third Avenue in Brooklyn. The clinic was in a squat brick building that sat under the elevated expressway alongside check cashing joints and scrap metal shops. It was 1980 and everything was grimy. The clinic had no windows, just bricked-in square sockets missing their square eyes—blind to the trouble it trafficked in Brooklyn. The roof was covered with curls of silver razor wire. Inside the front door sat a uniformed officer with a gun on his hip. But I liked working there. The clients served as an antidote for my own predilections. Their trauma flooded through the clinic and kept my own trauma at bay.

The first client I met in the clinic was Louis, a young guy my own age who tried hard to get clean. He dressed sharp every day and smelled of cologne. A Bengal tiger tattoo crouched at the crook of his arm, covering his troubled cradle of veins.

More than a third of adolescents who are abused or neglected will have a substance abuse disorder before they turn eighteen years old.

I took it hard when Louis disappeared. I took it hard when I learned that he had relapsed and was dying at home alone from a disease we'd soon learn to call AIDS.

The Guardian Angels had just begun patrolling the subways when I moved to New York City. They wore red berets and white T-shirts. The only weapons they carried were their martial arts skills and a cool logo bearing guardian wings. I decided to find a martial arts dojo in my Brooklyn neighborhood and begin my own training in earnest.

Most days after work, I headed over to the dojo eight blocks away. I kicked and screamed all over that place. The temple is a vulnerable spot on the body. I learned how to exploit it with a fast stab from an ink pen. I knew how to smash a nose with the heel of my hand and jab an eye with a finger turned bayonet. Everything can be made into a weapon somehow. The point is to shock the fucker and create enough space to just run away.

Several women in the dojo posted a manifesto in the dressing room and asked the other women to please sign the pledge:

I promise that should anyone ever attack me and try to rape me, I will always fight back with everything that I have, even if it means a fight to my death.

As though our martyrdom will be remembered and hailed in the future, our faces commemorated on postage stamps, and our sacrifice observed annually with large wreaths of white flowers.

Because not fighting to the death marks you for life as some kind of traitor.

I watched as students left the dressing room taller by a foot after making a promise to one another to never be me.

I put my hand on my heart and felt it beating—kung fu kung fu kung fu. The only thing I promised was to keep my traitorous story well undercover.

We've always had ways to describe the suffering that continues after nearly losing your life. *Soldier's heart* was the term used to describe post-traumatic stress disorder among Civil War veterans. *Shell shock* and *battle fatigue* were for veterans of fresher combat. Only recently have we realized that rape is the longest-running war on the planet.

Most of all it behooves us to take better care of one another.

I wanted to join a confederacy of Angels with black belts and red berets whose only promise was to help citizens travel safely on subways.

A friend from New Orleans who'd been to the Big Apple gave me some tips before I left the Big Easy.
Walk and talk faster than normal.
Keep your eyes open.
Sit next to other women on the trains after dark.

We sit next to each other under cities in tunnels, like friendly nations allied through battles. Our scarves and jackets pool around our neighboring borders.

Dear PTSD,
Please end the war.

Of course, it doesn't work that way. LBJ hadn't listened. Was there ever a world without a war?

Much later, when I think of risking my cover and sharing my story, I write another letter—this one from the man in the green pickup truck to me at my desk. He'll object, of course, to my version of the events.

Dear You,

Why call it rape? That's going too far. We both got away. Besides, don't forget, I was the only one out looking for you.

I never forget.

~~~

I DON'T remember the exact day my mother come back home from her summer road trip. But I know it was after I passed summer school algebra because I signed her name on my report card with big swirling loops the way she would have done. And I know it was after the Watergate hearings went off the air on August 8th because she missed the whole thing and I no longer came home in the afternoon to watch it live on our tiny Sony TV. I don't remember having to rush around and clean up the apartment. I always kept the dishes washed, the rugs vacuumed, the plants happy, and the bathroom clean.

I don't remember the day my mother returned, because she left again the following summer for five or six weeks, and that's what sticks out. I remember Mr. Rochester betraying Jane more clearly than I remember their reunion. I think that's just how memory works—like a camera zooming in to the parts that are on fire. But I can imagine my mother's silver Honda Z pulling up to the curb in front of our apartment with all her stuff in the back seat. And I imagine if I was home, I helped carry all her things back up to our place.

I don't remember, but I guess she had stories to share about the desert and the thousands of stars you can see in New Mexico when you're camping at night, and how she'd still like to fly into outer space if she had a rocket.

I imagine I helped my mom pack and unpack her silver Honda Z again the next summer.

One of the astronauts said that when they went to the moon, they were technicians, but when they returned to Earth, they were humanitarians. He was talking about the power of the big picture, the connections you can see from up and over, that view you get when you float in space like a dead man and look back at your home.

My mother went to New Mexico and then to Minnesota and around somewhere, but I was the one who got the long-distance view, like Jane and Caine and Tecumseh did. And just like them, I tried to love the whole world and its magnificent desolation, even if it killed me. See how much like a love story this is.

Part 7

Mathematics—from Ancient Greek (*máthēma*),
meaning *that which is learnt and what one gets to know.*

TO MAKE SENSE OF INFINITY, the heavens were divided into
houses and elements and given their own names. My first breath
was Libra, the sign of peace at all costs. The sign learning to balance and keep it together.

I picked up astrology in New York City. I read old texts in metaphysical bookstores and tried to decode the secret language of
planets.

The bottom of the sky, closest to earth, is where you'll find your
roots and your tribe and also your mother. Pisces swims through
my roots like an angel-seal hybrid. New Orleans swims through
my tribe a few feet below sea level.

My mother's confirmation name was Lucy, after Saint Lucy, the
patron saint of eyesight, a martyred saint whose eyeballs were
plucked out by her captors. Or else she plucked them out with her
own hands in protest. There are two different stories—either way,
she lost both her eyes.

In the church my mother attended as a child, there was a statue of
Lucy holding her own eyeballs in a small serving dish. The statue

terrified my mother. So, she chose Lucy's name as her own as a way to pluck out and tame any fear that she felt.

Lucy means *clear, bright, and understandable.* My mother gave me Clare as a middle name. Clare means *clear, bright, and understandable.* Saint Clare is the patron saint of sore eyes. The coincidences are accidental or else they are not. My mother and I are tethered together through our names and our skies and the bottom of our eyes.

~~~

I TOOK a yoga class in Brooklyn to help me relax after all the kicking and punching. The teacher would tell us in a voice like a dream to *feel your center, go at your own pace, be here and now inside of your body.*

In Sanskrit, the word "yoga" describes *a discipline that allows us to achieve a state of connection and mastery.* In other words, yoga is a kind of kung fu.

When I was in college, before yoga was a thing here in this country, my mother started teaching the yoga she knew on her living room floor. Whenever I came home for a visit, I'd take my place in her class. The best pose she taught me was the pose of a tree.

The teacher in Brooklyn ended each class with us all standing like in an orchard in her small studio. *Feel your limbs, feel your leaves . . . exhale through your roots.* I stood as a tree with the other trees in her class. I'd inhale and exhale and hum to myself what I remembered from the song "Desiderata"—*you are a child of the universe, no less than the trees and the stars . . .* the rest I forgot.

I went to an acupuncturist once a week to help me manage the stomachaches that followed me everywhere. The acupuncturist told me my element was wood and my stomach was winter. *Wood element people are built to climb mountains, and Do or Die is your motto.* She needled my Middle of Person and my Crooked Pond points. *Close your eyes and think of rain in your gulley. Think of love in your liver.* She turned on some music and turned off the lights. Then she left like the summer.

When my mother and I drove down the highway when I was a kid, and later on as adults, we used to sing "We Belong to a Mutual Admiration Society"—the Ethel Merman version between a mother and her grown daughter sung in two-part harmony:

The mom—*She says I'm beautiful and smart. I think that's she's a work of art.*

The daughter—*She says that I am heaven-sent and that I'm her fan club president.*

The mom—*I tell her I am proud of her. She says that she is prouderer.*

Both—*And that's the way we pass the time of day.*

Suzanne Pleshette played Emily Hartley on *The Bob Newhart Show* when I was in high school. I'd watch for my mother in Pleshette's black hair and blue eyes. The way she smiled and looked sideways during every episode. The way we all looked at Pleshette and got the person she pretended.

~~

MY MOTHER'S parents didn't make it into my childhood. I learned early on not to ask my mother about her roots or her history. The more I asked, the less I got. As my mother would tell me—*No one was proud to be an immigrant or an immigrant's daughter.* But she did allow that her father was from Ireland and her mother was from Spain. She did tell me that her parents met in the Catholic church, like so many other immigrants back then. I knew there were ten in her family all living together in a shotgun house on Music Street. The front stoop was their bonus room, and the St. Roch neighborhood was their turf.

Trees survive because of a complex system of roots that are so intertwined we could stride right across them if need be and never fall through. This underground network serves as a marketplace for all the trees in the area. A Douglas fir on one side may drink less so that an at-risk maple sapling miles away gets more food. Who knew?

My mother was the best tree I could see. She was my taproot and canopy. I knew there had to be more to our story, maybe underground. I turned into a mole and dug for connections, because even a child of the universe wants to have roots.

My mother's one sister lived out-of-state. She was younger than my mother and just as silent about their past. One of my mother's favorite brothers traveled most of the year working on rigs for Shell Oil Company. Her other favorite brother lived on the run until he was caught and did time in prison. My mother described the rest of her brothers as ice-cold. All in all, no one was talking. In the stories my mother did tell, her father was her tree and her mother was her trouble. I dug for the tree.

Everything I learned about my grandfather, in chronological order over the course of a lifetime:

1. That he was James Thomas Cunningham from County Kerry, Ireland, who came to this country when he was in his late teens.

2. That he was so happy to have a baby girl, after so many sons. That he brought his workmates home to look at my newborn mother as she lay in her crib.

3. That when my mother had nightmares, he told her to call him into the dream and he would appear and protect her.

4. That each year he drew a Christmas tree on three feet of brown wrapping paper and hung it on the inside of the front door. That it looked magical. That my mother made ornaments for the one-dimensional tree from tin foil candy wrappers.

5. That he was an electrician.

6. That he was not an electrician. That he was a janitor. That he worked in the boiler room of an office building in downtown New Orleans and lost his job

and was an alcoholic and one of his older sons had to
carry him home each night on his back. (This I found
out from one of the ice-cold brothers when he was in
the hospital high on painkillers and close to death.
Someone needs to know the truth, he said to the mole.)

7. That he shot himself behind his house after lunch
   one day after walking around the dining room table
   and tussling the curly black hair of his two lovely
   daughters. That my mother was seventeen at the
   time, pregnant, newly married to a tap dancer who
   moved into their crowded place on Music Street.
   That my mother miscarried after her father's shot
   to the head. That my mother's new husband left her
   not long after she lost her father and then lost her
   baby.

8. That the family was able to get special dispensation
   to bury James Thomas Cunningham in the Catholic
   part of a New Orleans cemetery.

The top four on the list were the good news. I had a grandfather
who practiced dream yoga and cherished his girls. The rest of the
list shook the roots of my heart for my little girl mother.

No photos of my grandfather survived, but my mother said he had
black hair and blue eyes just like she did. I pretended him into our
living room too. And sometimes at night, I would feel him tussle
my hair when I was home on my own and falling asleep.

Interdependence is a thing we barely understand.

Several portraits of Tecumseh, painted when he was alive, have
survived all the way forward in time. In some paintings he wears
a brigadier's blue jacket. A feather hangs from the cloth wrapped
around his head. He has long hair and strong eyes. Even now when
I see the evening's first star, I think of Tecumseh and the way he
showed up just when I needed.

Most of all, it behooves us to take each other in.

Why, it's almost like being in love . . .

~~

I KNEW an old man in New York City who picked up every penny and coin he found on the ground. He was a refugee from Tibet. He couldn't believe these Americans who stepped right over the very thing they worked so hard to collect.

Pure merit, pure value, he'd tell his grown children, who would roll their eyes whenever he'd stop in the middle of a crosswalk or grocery store aisle to pick up a penny. *Think something good,* he would tell them.

Once I started, I saw coins everywhere, mostly pennies. I collected them all like the man from Tibet. I put them in the red British telephone booth bank I kept on my kitchen counter. I'd watch the coins pile up through the booth's mini square windows. On a good year, the bank was jam-packed by December, and I'd have to use a jar for the overflow of coins.

My mother collected silver dimes her whole life. She liked their little thin size. After 1965, dimes were sandwiched with copper. She'd pass me the change from the cashier after shopping and have me sort through the coins for any dimes that were all silver. She tucked them away for safekeeping in a little black change purse in the back of her drawer. I felt like her prospector partner panning for a way to increase my net worth.

Over the course of one year, I found a 1919 solid silver Mercury dime, a walking Liberty quarter, over twenty dollars' worth of pennies, quarters, and dimes, dozens of dropped earrings, and several dollar bills. I had a total of $31.15—a record year since I began counting. I drove to an intersection near the shopping mall where a man stood holding a small cardboard sign that read PLEASE HELP! NOTHING IS 2 SMALL! in blue Magic Marker. I thought something good and gave him the merit.

Part 8

A teardrop of green.

—RON MCNAIR, NASA ASTRONAUT

EVER SINCE CAINE on *Kung Fu* seared his forearms with dragons, I wanted to get a tattoo of my own. The artist in the tattoo parlor asked me twice if I was sure of myself. Not many women in the late 1970s sported tattoos on their arms. But like Caine, I wanted a secret badge I could always keep with me. I sat down in the tattoo artist's chair with my right arm exposed. A dragon with the wings of a phoenix came to live on my shoulder. Like Caine, I've kept her under my sleeve as a creature whose history only I understand.

I dreamed one night that I had another tattoo—red, black, and blue designs swirled over the right side of my face. In the dream it was clear that I'd always had the tattoo and had just learned not to see it. I was shaken to look in the dream mirror and see the marks I couldn't disguise cover half of my face.

I picked at the red lines that swirled down my neck and up over one eyebrow like tendrils of ivy. Most of them peeled off with some effort, but a block of black on my cheek and a swoosh of blue down my chin were marks that would never come off until the next life or the one after that.

Pretend I'm not here.

On *This American Life*, a guy asks another guy to choose between two superpowers—invisibility or flight. I was sure they'd choose flight. But the two men on the podcast wanted to slip around in the world as invisible voyeurs. *What could be better?* they asked one another. *Wings!* I shouted to the guys on the radio—men who were never pretended away, who see themselves clearly in a world that sees them, who could go dark with their powers and still retain all their worldly advantage. What could be better?

Is it my story that marks me or the telling that does it?

I can tell you this—right before my father left, before I was six, I dreamed I was lost from my mother. The whole dream was too dark, and my panic was a fire. Then right before dawn she was pushed into my view in a baby doll carriage holding a bottle. Her limbs sprawled over the sides and her eyes were dead doll blue.

See how I floated ahead of myself and tried to get ready?

~~~

AFTER I got home that Thursday night, sometime after midnight, and stood shaking in the bathroom trying to change out of my clothes and wash blood off my legs, I picked up the phone and called Gifford. I don't remember what I said when he answered the phone, but I remember everything sounding far away in a tunnel. I waited on the porch until his sky-blue VW bug pulled up. I got into his car. I don't know what I thought he would do, but his twenty-nine years felt better than my skinny fourteen. His car felt safer than my empty apartment and his face felt better in my eyes than the afterimages I was left with.

We'll find him, he said.
    What? I asked.
    Open the glove compartment.

I don't know what I expected to find, but not a gun.

Zoom in Zoom out.

The gun was a bright silver pistol with a pearl-white handle, and it looked just like a heftier version of the cowboy cap gun I had when I was nine.

Is it real? I asked.
Gifford nodded.
He drove us around the park. It was my second tour around the park that night with a man and his weapon. I didn't want to find the red-haired man and his green pickup truck. I didn't look for the red-haired man and his green pickup truck. When Gifford touched my shoulder to see if I was all right, I jumped and grabbed the door handle. He let me out in front of my place.

Don't be scared.

After that Thursday I could hear everything at night. I listened to my eyelashes scrape across the pillowcase. After midnight, after the traffic noise settled down, after I hadn't fallen asleep again, I could hear the rumble of the streetcars four blocks away. There were only two streetcars on the tracks after midnight. I would lie in my bed and listen as they orbited each other on Saint Charles Avenue.

My feet took it hard. Most nights they were restless under the covers, kicking the way they had wanted to kick. Smashing kneecaps, running rabbit-fast. They had screamed in that truck, but only I could hear them.

After nights of setting up my alarm of pots and ashtrays, I sat on Gifford's streetcar as we moved down the humid avenue into the late hours—slow and not alone anymore. Then he brought me to his place. He combed my hair and made me a sandwich and took me to his bed. And I listened to Stevie Wonder *blame it on the sun* as I floated above us, counterclockwise in the dark space of the room.

Men can't understand rape.

For every living thing there is a different solution. A different way of staying alive.

Gifford picked me up sometimes and took me to the lakefront. I remember wearing a new knitted maroon top I found in my mother's closet. Gifford had the night off from work. The sun had just set, and he'd stopped on the way for a bag of boiled shrimp. I wasn't hungry, but he was. He wanted me to eat with him. He wanted me to sleep with him. Nothing felt like sleeping anymore.

I liked the mornings better, when Gifford drove me to summer school, and he kissed me before I got out of his Volkswagen Beetle. He bought me a cinnamon roll to eat on the way because he knew I wasn't eating much, and he knew I liked cinnamon.

Best were the days Gifford just wanted someone to ride along with him. We drove to the University of New Orleans campus to deliver some documents from the Veterans Administration for a class he was taking. We drove to the dry cleaners to drop off the blue suit he wore to church on Sundays with the grandmother who raised him. We went to an amusement park, and he bought me soft ice cream swirled into an extra-large cone.

Other times he made me go in the drugstore and buy him condoms while he sat in the car and watched me. If I didn't go into the store and get him the condoms, he'd make me go home all alone. Sometimes he'd wake me up again and again to have sex with him and one more time before I left for school. He never seemed to be finished with me.

Once or twice Gifford took me to a motel under an overpass in a bad part of town. He left me there after the sex part was over. I jammed the back of a chair under the doorknob like I'd seen in the movies. I stacked the two glass ashtrays I found in the bathroom against the front of the door like I did at home. I put the motel room phone in the bed right beside me. I can't remember why we were in that danger motel or why he left me there all on my own. I only remember that I held it together and when he returned in the morning I was so happy to see him.

Not telling isn't always a decision. Not telling becomes a way of life. The way your heart cave becomes a loaded glove compartment.

For decades, if I tell anyone any part of my story, I will skim over the all-alone factor. I will skip the Gifford part altogether. Because how do you describe what you cannot yet really see? The love and abuse all mixed together like water and milk. Which one is which? The *I don't want to do this* with *I don't want to lose this*.

This the only person to show up and help.

Later on, when I cannot not see the parts I skipped over before, I write a poem in three stanzas—the aggravated part, the statutory part, and the part that was neglected.

I read this poem to a small group of writers for feedback one night over glasses of wine and cups of black coffee. Mostly, they get it. They see that neglect was the engine that pulled the other parts forward. They see the landscape of a target and the range of a predator. But one writer points to the statutory stanza and voices the voice I've carried for years—that my *neediness* caused the whole awful mess. She looks down at me in three parts on the page while I sit in my chair and burn like a traitor.

This one had cool blue sheets and said he loved me. This one combed my hair and burned musk incense and used a condom and wasn't a redneck with a jackhammer of pink hate. We smoked African weed. We listened to Stevie Wonder.

And I floated counterclockwise like a lost girl in the dark lagoon of the room.

Part 9

Your body belongs to the revolution.
So, you must take care of it.

—THE 1970S

AFTER THE MAN IN THE TRUCK, and sleeping with Gifford, there had been a furious burning. Lucky for me, there was a doctor in the house—a 400-page paperback home medical reference that sat on the bookshelf in the living room. I followed my symptoms and found *Trichomoniasis: a sexually transmitted disease often caused by having multiple sexual partners. Sometimes referred to as "the trich." Trich* was pronounced *trick*. I looked up *rape* in the 400-page paperback home medical reference. What I found was nothing. No symptoms or causes or cures. No home remedies. No suggestions about what to do next.

The home medical reference did state that trichomoniasis was easily curable with one course of antibiotics prescribed by a doctor. This was good news, unless, of course, you were fourteen years old and needed a doctor who would treat you for free, who would not ask how old you were, who would not care how you came to have multiple sexual encounters at such a young age, who would not ask where one of your multiple parenting people was, who would not tell anyone anything you didn't want shared.

Julie and I sat on folding chairs in the hallway of the St. Mark's Community Center on North Rampart Street where the HEAD

Clinic was located. The HEAD (Health Emergency Aid Dispensary) Clinic was set up to help street people and stray hippies and anyone else who couldn't get medical care because they couldn't find enough money.

Two doctors walked down the hallway toward us. They didn't look like doctors. They just looked like two guys who might hang out in the park with us and our friends. They wore blue jeans and T-shirts under their white lab coats. One had a scraggly dark beard and looked like Cat Stevens. The other one had a medium Afro and looked like Jimi Hendrix.

Are you waiting for a doctor? the Cat Stevens one asked.
Yes, I said. I showed him the clinic's informational card I had picked up at the library.
Are you here for a gynecological issue?
I nodded.
Cat Stevens handed the HEAD card back to me. *We're not seeing patients right now. I'm sorry.*

There are many stories of mountain climbers who are lost for days, who defy the odds and the elements and make it back to base camp only to die in a warm tent during the night. Their mistake was to think they were safe and home free. They relaxed and they died. Better to stay ready if you want to keep living.

Base camp had packed up and left the mountain without me. I stared at their shoes walking away—one pair of white Converse sneakers and one pair of brown leather sandals like mine.

The 400-page paperback medical reference listed a home remedy for trichomoniasis—*douche with vinegar and warm water*. I looked up the word *douche* in the dictionary. I searched through the kitchen pantry and found a bottle of white vinegar.

We all want to escape.—Houdini

Like everything else, I figured it out on my own. In college, I was given a course of antibiotics when I had the flu, and it cured the whole mess.

Some nights during that summer when I couldn't sleep, I would stand on the back porch and search for the moon. Then I'd absorb all her moonlight. Even when she was cut in half and flying far away from me.

Part 10

You can't just see a tree as a stand-alone character anymore.

—DR. NALINI NADKARNI

HER NAME WAS TIFFANY, and she was fourteen years old. She was just about my height. I recognized the way she sat very still and scoped out the room and everyone in it. Like me, she was built to climb mountains. Sink or swim was her motto.

Fifteen of us sat around a collection of folding tables that had been pushed together in a U-shaped formation. We filled the conference room at a family services office in a neighboring county. The North Carolina Department of Child Protective Services had removed Tiffany from her mother's care 925 days earlier—well beyond the one-year goal of a permanent placement. My job as a family mediator was to facilitate a discussion about options and next steps. The presiding judge was hoping the parties would agree on those next steps in mediation and avoid a court hearing.

I felt for the flat rock I kept in my pocket as a small bit of ballast during difficult mediations. A piece of the earth to help me come back to myself after walking around in the shoes of the others.

Tiffany noticed the dark clouds peeking out from the bottom of my short-sleeve shirt. I was surprised since I'd chosen the shirt because it normally covered my entire tattoo. The clouds must have appeared as I leaned forward with my elbows on the table and talked with her.

Can I see it? she asked me.

I lifted my sleeve.

Cool. Is it a bird? What kind of bird?

It's mostly a phoenix, I said.

I told her the myth of the phoenix. She was going to need it.

Tiffany's mother was in another room, conferring with her court-appointed attorney and her guardian ad litem. We were all taking a break while we waited for them to return. The other professionals checked their cell phones and traded weekend plans with each other.

I'm going to tattoo my mother's name on my right arm and my sister's name on my other arm, Tiffany said to me.

I didn't know you have a sister, I said.

I haven't seen her since I was nine. She won't claim me because I am full black and she's half.

Oh, I said.

This is what it is—we tattoo ourselves with the people who won't claim us.

She pointed at the soft side of her wrist. *And right there, I'm going to get the infinity symbol tattooed with the word "infinity" written in script underneath it.*

Huh, I said. *How come?*

I really like how infinity looks.

Me, too.

She took a black marker from the whiteboard behind us and drew the sideways eight across the belly of her left wrist. I wondered if Tiffany and I were synonyms of each other or if all fourteen-year-olds have a thing for infinity.

She tapped my arm. *Hey, your name and my name are kind of alike. Tiffany. Stephanie. You know what I'm saying?*

I nodded.

Sometimes they call me Tiff, for short. Sometimes they call me Tough.

Me, too, I said.

Tiffany looked over at me and smiled. The only smile I would see that day.

Tiffany rested her hands palm up on the table and admired her temporary tattoo. I looked at her hands and I looked at my hands.

I'd read somewhere that if you think you might be in the middle of a dream, stop everything and look at your hands. If you are dreaming, colors will swirl across your palms, and you will have the chance to become lucid. It's true. I tried this once and my hands went crazy with paisleys of yellow and green.

Our hands didn't change. Mine, all tough, and hers, fourteen.

Tiffany's mother and her attorney came back into the conference room. Her mother sat on the other side of Tiffany and stroked Tiffany's arm, the arm that would one day bear her name. Around the table sat agency attorneys, parent attorneys, caseworkers, guardians ad litem, Tiffany, her mother, her mother's cousin, the therapeutic foster mother, my co-mediator, and me.

After 925 days, Tiffany's mother had two options left—fight the termination of her parental rights, or allow the therapeutic foster parent to adopt Tiffany. Tiffany's mother stood a better chance of staying connected to Tiffany if she chose the second option. Her attorney had explained this to her in their private meeting.

After 925 days, everyone except Tiffany could see that her mother's chances weren't as good with door number one. Everyone could see the benefits for Tiffany of being raised by her therapeutic foster mother while keeping a connection with her actual mother. Even her mother, who had been found to have a *diminished capacity* and was impaired to the point that she had her own guardian ad litem and who sat at the table wearing a sweatshirt, pajama bottoms, and gray and pink bedroom slippers each shaped like a mouse, saw it as well. The professionals around the table leaned back and relaxed as Tiffany's mother stepped closer to the option of voluntary relinquishment. Tiffany and I still leaned forward in our chairs, looking at our hands, contemplating eternity.

Tiffany's mother's attorney asked for a smaller meeting so his client could talk with her daughter. He asked that the guardians ad litem and mediators be present. As we walked into the hallway, Tiffany pulled me to the side. We stood in the corner in front of a bookcase full of pamphlets for new parents.

Why is this called neglect? she asked me. *The Bible says God will give you everything you need—food, clothing, shelter. My mom gave me all that. She even brought me to the hospital once when I was sick. She always fed me, and she never left me alone. Other people do worse—way worse. Why call this neglect?*

I brought her guardian ad litem advocate and the guardian ad litem attorney back to the bookcase in the corner to answer Tiffany's questions. The attorney fiddled with his notepad and looked at me as he spoke to her.

Well, when a parent allows dangerous people into the house and when a parent doesn't make good decisions for their child, it can also be called neglect.
　　Tiffany shrugged. *I want her to fight for me.*
　　The advocate patted Tiffany's arm. *Tiffany, you are doing so well. If you graduate from high school, the state will help you with in-state college tuition, just like we talked about. You can have something better. You can be the person you want to be.*

Tiffany looked at me. I was pretty sure she wanted to be a person with a mother who was up to the task of mothering her.
　　I pointed to a door at the end of the hall where we were supposed to join Tiffany's mother and her attorney.
　　You don't have to go, I said.
　　No, Tiffany said. *I want to.*
　　I followed a few feet behind Tiffany. I could feel me feeling her.
　　I overheard someone whisper to the attorney behind me—*These kids always protect the mom to the same degree they were not protected.*
　　It's a thing, I wanted to say. *I'd like to know what you would do floating around on the dark side of the moon all by yourself.*

Tiffany and I and the guardians ad litem walked into the small room. The room usually served as a playroom for children. A colorful carpet covered the floor and Dr. Seuss books were stacked in a pile on a miniature table. The lawyer had dragged a few adult-sized chairs in from the hallway. I sat next to a rocking chair where a pink bear was sitting. Tiffany handed me the bear and sat down beside me. Across the small room sat her mother, flanked by her attorney and her own guardian ad litem.

The attorney cleared his throat. *Tiffany, your mother wants to talk with you before signing these papers.*

Her mother held a box of tissues close to her chest. I wanted to pair her up with the pink bear so they'd at least have one another. Both of them stared off into space with round glassy eyes. Their large fuzzy feet were stretched out in front as they waited for a child to come and collect them.

Her mother sobbed. *Tiff, I did everything I could. I did everything, Baby.* She caught her breath and started again. *Everything I could, everything. I did, I did.*

Her mother looked at me and looked at Tiffany. Tiffany sat in the rocking chair, frozen and careful.

Do you want to sit next to your mom? I asked.

She nodded and changed places with the guardian. She put her arm around her mother, like a mother would. And her mother fell apart in her arms, like a child would.

I knew that for Tiffany, this was better than nothing at all. I looked over at my co-mediator. He stared off into the space between them and us. For me it was too late. There was no neutral space left.

I walked Tiffany out of the small room. The attorney and guardian stayed in the room to help her mother through all the paperwork required for the voluntary relinquishment of her parental rights. Someone called a local notary to come over and formally witness the event. I wondered if they would list a time of termination, the way a time of death is formally listed on a death certificate.

Tiffany and I walked back into the large conference room where everyone else waited. A few people were on their phones, the rest were talking with each other about vacation plans. Tiffany asked me if she could draw on the whiteboard.

We found a set of colorful markers. Each marker was loaded with its own fruity scent to go with its color. I stood at the board while Tiffany drew a field of green grass along with a stand of thin trees. Soon everything around us smelled like sour apples. I waited to see if she would take the brown marker and unleash dark chocolate roots, but does anyone draw roots?

Is this really neglect? she asked me again. *She loves me, you know.*
  I know, I said.
  I knew her questions because I had asked her questions. My astrologer friends had looked at my chart and tried to answer my questions. *You have a right to be here*, they'd said.

I'd sat in my mediator disguise in conference rooms like this one all across the state. I'd listened to attorneys parse the definitions of neglect and abandonment and the combinations of both.

Neglect is when a parent fails to provide what a child needs to such a degree that the child is at risk of harm. Serious neglect is when the harm occurs. And abandonment is when the parent's whereabouts are unknown, or the parent has failed to maintain contact with the child.

I'd sat in my mediator chair surprised no one else could hear my fourteen-year-old defender rise up from the ashes, again and again, chanting—*She loves me, you know. She loves me.*

I wanted to tell Tiffany—*There's no going home, but you have a right to be here.* I wanted to root down into that answer. I wanted to inhale it and exhale it and share it with her.

But I had less than two minutes before we'd get interrupted, and I had less than that to come up with a short answer. Even before I spoke, the answer sounded lame.

If I was put in the pilot's seat of a jet plane, I would not be able to fly that plane no matter how much I tried and no matter how much I loved the passengers. Right?

Tiffany nodded. Her face was soft as she absorbed all of my words.

It's kind of like that, I went on. *Your mom has agreed that your foster mom should fly the plane. But you still get to love your mom and she gets to love you. And you can have her in your life.*

The notary walked into the conference room.

I'm sorry, I told Tiffany. *I know it's just hard. I know it doesn't make much sense to you now.*

Tiffany nodded her head and blinked back tough tears. She looked through the trees she had drawn on the board and stared off into the empty white space.

Tiffany asked to go back to the small classroom and say goodbye to her mother. She wanted to mother her mother. She wanted to reassure her mother that she'd call her next week as soon as she was given her very own cell phone. She was worried that her mother might feel neglected.

In my office at work, I've had a Mutts cartoon tacked to my bulletin board for several years. A big bulldog with a spiked collar is chained to a stake in a yard. He can move only a few feet in any direction. Birds fly over him. One crow has landed in his yard and the bulldog has stretched to the end of his short chain so he can pat the crow on its head. He has a big bulldog grin all over his face. The quote in the sky above the dog reads—*You cannot always **have** happiness, but you can always **give** happiness.—Anonymous*

Mostly, I like how the dog has found a way to be connected to happiness. But sometimes I get mad when I look at the crow who is free to fly away anytime. That crow who has everything and still takes from the dog. That dog who's locked up on a short chain and still gives to the bird—while no one pats his big bulldog head.

Tiffany said goodbye to the impaired mother and walked out of the room with the therapeutic mother. I stood by the front door and said goodbye to each person as they left. Tiffany leaned forward and hugged me. I blinked back tough tears as one fell down her cheek. I knew that Tiffany would feel as though she was the one who had walked out on her mother and left her there forever falling apart.

I wanted to tell Tiffany that she'd already survived all the definitions of neglect. That it's keeping body and soul together that counts. Like a yogi, like a phoenix, like a kung fu master alone in the Wild West. We are both part of that tribe.

You cannot always have protection, but you can always give protection.

The other mediator and I said goodbye to each other and headed to our separate cars. I drove the 100 miles back to my office in Raleigh. I cried half the way home while the sun sank to its knees.

Part II

KATRINA HIT THE GULF COAST on a Monday morning, a moon day, and at first we thought we got lucky—the roof of the Superdome, the bridge over Lake Pontchartrain, the electricity to the city, these things could be fixed.

When you live in New Orleans, you get used to quick getaways during hurricane season. Two or three nights, if you can, if you have a car that can, and then back into town after the storm makes a name for itself over in Texas or fizzles out in the Gulf of Mexico in a swirl of salt water. You never pack your bags as if this is the one that will overwhelm all your roots.

My mother was seventy-eight when she left New Orleans for the middle of the state with a few clothes and her knitting in an overnight bag. She had one check in her checkbook. I called her during my lunch break at work from my job in the courthouse in downtown Raleigh. Her words came out slowly, but there was relief in her voice.

By Monday evening, the city was sinking on national TV. All week I watched as my homeland went under and all week tears pooled at the bottom of my sky.

Before we were called the Big Easy, we were nicknamed the City That Care Forgot. Some people think it means the same thing—as in put your cares away and come have a party. But others of us know the flip side of the name means we're always forgotten, after the party, when catastrophe hits. Sometimes, like Michael Collins, we're even famous for it.

If I had the superpower of flight, I could have flown into New Orleans and rescued some people. Even if I didn't have super-powerful arms, I could have picked up a few skinny people and lots of the pets and flown in and out of the city before the storm hit, or after the storm hit. Even if I had to make thousands of trips, that would have been a powerful thing.

Unless a name clearly says what it means—like a *June* or a *Joy*—we've mostly forgotten the original meaning. This is what the name Katrina means on the website I found: *Katrina is excitable or unflappable with extremes in fortune, health, and spirituality. She knows great success or abject misery. The solution is service to others.*

The solution is to stand with a foot on each extreme side and balance the story. If anyone had asked me, I could have told them that the unflappable part would be hard to master.

The half-duplex rental, where my mother lived, was close to the Mississippi River, whose levee held fast. The Pontchartrain levee is what broke apart and let loose the lake all over town. When the water receded, most of New Orleans and all of its beings were turned inside out all over the streets. The cleanup would be long, just like the mourning.

So many had died. Some came back home and others moved on. The returned dragged their refrigerators full of dead food out to the curb. They bound them shut with long strips of black tape. The fridges stood at attention curbside for miles, like an army of zombies waiting for their general to arrive. Rotting food and maggots leaked from their taped seams. Some of them sported black graffiti tattoos.

Smells like FEMA
Make Levees Not War
Bush & Mayor Nagin's Lunch Inside

There was no going home for my mother—not in the same way, just like her friends who were too old to return. She was able to get some of her belongings before she moved in with me in North Carolina.

~~~

THE YEAR before Katrina, my mother had begun struggling to get the words she wanted to say out of her mouth. She could go for a day or two without any hitch, but then it would come back, and every other word came out upside down and all over the place.

I flew back home to New Orleans a couple of times that year to help my mother with doctor's appointments. She thought it might have something to do with her chronic sinusitis. She thought her sinuses were somehow stealing her speech right off the tip of her tongue. I hoped it was true. These things could be fixed.

Doctors looked at my mother's sinuses and found nothing wrong there. A neurologist was the next doctor on her list. Before she could see him, Katrina drowned all her medical records and upcoming appointments. We had to start over when she moved in with me.

The gerontologist looked over the test results from the Duke neurology clinic. He agreed with the diagnosis—my mother had small vessel disease of the brain. *Why call it dementia*, he said when I asked. *Dementia just means a degree of confusion. Aren't we all confused now and then?*

I was totally confused. So was my mother.

There are a hundred different kinds of dementia, the woman at the front desk of the local Alzheimer's Association told me. *Small vessel disease of the brain is a cause of vascular dementia. Vascular dementia is like the lady and the tiger. You'll never know which one your mother is when she walks in the door.*

She loaded me up with a binder of information and a directory of local resources. She tossed in some pamphlets she pulled off the display rack in the wood-paneled lobby.

Knowledge is a kind of power, she said.

The doctors haven't given me half this much power, I said.

She opened the front door for me and patted my arm as I walked by carrying my stack of homework.

You are not alone, she said.

You are not not alone, I said aloud in my car.

I set the homework in the passenger's seat and drove home. When I got home, I put the binder and directory and pamphlets on the top shelf of my closet under my sweatshirts. I didn't pull it down from the shelf for over a year. In that year, I searched for an adult day care center that seemed like a good fit. I searched for a caregiver support group to attend. I found out how to secure power of attorney for what lay ahead. After a year, I pulled down the not-alone binder and flipped open to page 1.

What I learned from the dementia caregivers support group:

- Pick your battles. Save your breath. Let it go.

- *Therapeutic lying* sounds like a contradiction, but actually it's a solution. Just like *aikido,* a martial art that doesn't use hitting or kicking.

    ai—joining, unifying

    ki—spirit, mood

    dō—way, path

    Therapeutic lying joins you to the spirit and mood of the confused so you can redirect them on their path without fighting and stress.

- Caregivers often die from the stress of the task, and all the joining and unifying involved in the task, before the patient dies from their dementia.

~~~

SELECTIVE BRAIN *filtering* isn't directly related to vascular dementia, but the name came up with the other results of my online search for more information. I clicked on the link and watched a video featuring six people—three in white shirts and three in black shirts bouncing basketballs while a fake gorilla walked right through the mad throng. You don't see the gorilla if you are following the instructions and counting the dribbles versus the passes of the trio in white shirts. Not even when the gorilla mugs for the camera and waves a few times. But my mother, whose brain wasn't filtering much anymore, waved and laughed while I sat in the chair still counting the dribbles.

In the early days of her dementia, we'd sit together on the couch in my guest room in North Carolina. The guest room was her room since Hurricane Katrina forced her to move in. We'd watch *Lost* on TV every Wednesday evening. After half a dozen episodes, we couldn't follow the storyline anymore. Survivors of a plane crash were stuck in a tropical limbo land with monsters made of smoke. All of them started to question reality.

Why call it lost when everyone is confused? It's just a matter of degree.

We aren't alone, I told my mother.

~~~

IN THE middle days of her dementia, I saw way more of the tiger and less of the lady. If I could get her to sleep by ten, I would sit alone in my room with the light turned down low, a bowl of Cheerios on my lap, and watch *Locked Up Abroad* on cable TV. After years in captivity, each person each week was eventually sent back to their country. And each week, for years, I'd feel a rush of second-hand freedom while locked up at home.

The day came when I looked at my passport and laughed out loud. Long gone were the days when an official document with a seal from the government had the power to transport me out of captivity. I looked at the small photo of myself from an earlier time and laughed at my hair, my eager expression, the gorillas I could now see just over my shoulder.

~~~

EVERY NIGHT, while my mother ate her scrambled egg dinner, I went into her room and began the therapeutic alarm clock lie. I moved the hands ahead one hour on the chance she would believe me when I said it was time to turn off the lights and go to sleep. After she fell asleep, I'd tiptoe into her room and turn the hands of the clock back two hours, on the chance she would look at the clock when she woke up multiple times in the middle of the night and decide to stay in bed for a change.

As a teenager, I would have given anything for my mother to be a light sleeper and wake up easy-peasy. As a caregiver, I would have given anything for my mother to fall into a deep sleep and stay there for eight hours.

My mother and I had alarm clock karma. Patterns are everywhere, like all the ways I was always in charge.

The alarm clock lie only worked for a month.

~~~

THE DEMENTIA caregiver support group was more like an emergency huddle that met twice a month. We gathered downtown in a meeting room at the Methodist church. The room was carefully appointed with couches and coffee tables and a large grandfather clock that stood in the corner.

Judy was our coach. She had a smoker's laugh and wore holiday sweaters with snowflakes in the winter and pink Myrtle Beach T-shirts during the summer. Judy had retired after directing the adult day care in the church basement below us—the day care my mother attended Monday through Friday while I was at work. During each meeting we pumped Judy for every caregiving tip she had left in her. And each meeting she fed us warm homemade cookies that we inhaled like crack.

After work or after the support group meeting, I'd go to the church basement to pick up my mother. Half the time her face was a furious pink storm. She'd point to the clock on the wall and glare at me—certain I was late or had forgotten all about her. Of course, I'd never been late, not even one time. *You have to be kidding me?* I wanted to shout at the woman who had forgotten all about me so many times. But she had tears in her eyes. I gave her a cookie and helped her into my car.

Oh, vascular dementia, Judy said. *Have you heard about the lady and the tiger?*

I nodded.

It's like that. So, your mom can't talk or process things well, but she knows who you are. And Mike's wife, who has forgotten who he is, can talk up a storm.

Mike took an oatmeal cookie and nodded. His wife had early onset Alzheimer's disease. He told us how every morning, for the last thirty years, he'd made breakfast for the two of them. They'd listen to the news on the radio and then head out to their separate jobs. But now after his wife ate the French toast and drank the hot tea that he'd made her, she would look up and say—*I know you, right? I love you, right?*

~~

MY MOTHER wanted to see *How the Brain Works* at our Museum of Natural Sciences. Even with a damaged brain, my mother would scan the newspaper each morning and find things I never saw. She'd tear them out and hand them to me as I rushed off to work. That's how we ended up visiting the traveling brain show together.

We walked under a bundle of nerves that lit up over our heads. We walked all the way around a two-story brain. We watched kids play a game with tubes and balls that supposedly demonstrated how neurons work, but the kids threw the balls at each other instead. They shouted into the tubes, and like an impromptu theater act, they demonstrated to us how neurons afflicted with dementia might work.

I'm a dancer, my mother said. *I know . . . to work work . . . my body. My brain . . . doesn't . . . dizzle . . . I dot don't . . . how . . .* she tapped her temple and turned away. We went into the science café and ate freeze-dried Neapolitan ice cream, the kind that astronauts eat while stuck in a space station spinning between stars. And I shivered with the fact that no matter what I did, I couldn't steer us back toward our green planet Earth.

~~~

MICHAEL SHERMER of *Skeptic* magazine coined the word *patternicity*. He defined *patternicity* as *the tendency to find meaningful patterns in meaningless noise.* The error of seeing something that is not there. In other words, *a false positive.*

Shermer's math isn't wrong, but patterns have kept us alive as hunters and gatherers—and as girls getting by in the world full of noise. *Is that sound behind me just the wind in the woods? Or is it a wolf?* Wrong decision and you're gone like the wind. Most of the time, the noise is a wolf.

For some people, Mother Mary's positive image appeared in the pattern of stains on the side of an overpass in downtown Chicago. And on the reflective glass of an office building in Clearwater, Florida. And sometimes just in the sky overhead, where a few children felt her feeling them in Bosnia Herzegovina before the war started.

I'm no Catholic (except by osmosis), but isn't Mary the wind?

~~~

MY MOTHER pointed to her teeth and grimaced.
    Do you have a toothache? I asked.
    She nodded.

I'll make an appointment with my dentist, Dr. Jones. You'll like him.

I helped my mother get situated in the dentist's chair and then went to the restroom. When I returned, Dr. Jones was standing in front of my mother with his hand behind his back. He looked like he was performing a magic trick for her. I looked at my mother and there was the trick—her face had collapsed. My mother's mouth had caved in, and her teeth were all gone. Then there were her teeth in Dr. Jones's hand.

How long has she had dentures? he asked me.

I would find out later that all my mother's teeth were extracted when she was a young woman and went to see a dentist, probably for the first time. That was the best-case scenario when you grew up poor during the Great Depression. She slept with her dentures in her mouth every night of her life. And every day of her life she hid the fact that her teeth weren't her own.

⌒⌒

THE MOM and daughter—*I think she's absolutely great. She says, oh that's a family trait.*
The mom—*I say that kind of flattery will get you any place with me . . .*
Both—*And that is how we'll still be years from now.*

⌒⌒

DURING THE middle of my mother's dementia, I took her to a double feature at the IMAX theater in downtown Raleigh. The first show was *Hubble 3D*, and I knew she would like it. The extreme screen went black and then stars appeared all around us. We floated fast past Saturn's aurora.

Ooooooooohhhhhhh, my mother said.

We toured the Pillars of Creation, where new stars are born in gas and clouds of ancient dust. Turns out stars sing if you have special equipment to pick up their wavelengths.

I didn't like the feeling of floating so far from Earth. I took off the 3D glasses and the Pillars went flat. The screen looked more like the most recent MRI image of my mother's brain. The misshapen circles of blurry light were the places where small blood vessels had closed. Maybe new stars and a new life were incubating in her pillar of old dust.

The film left me cold, but my mother was jazzed. She pointed at the screen and then at herself, and I knew she was trying to tell me that she would have been happy to have lived in the Hubble.

The next film was *Van Gogh: Brush with Genius*. We traveled through colors from Amsterdam to the south of France. I put the 3D glasses back on and warmed up near Arles in Van Gogh's high yellow note. We floated through blossoming chestnut trees and a wheat field with Crows. Somewhere along the way, Van Gogh lost his mind and painted a sky full of bipolar stars.

The number of nights that my mother circled through the house like a lost satellite only increased. We'd sleep for an hour or two in between orbits. The mornings after were catastrophes of crying jags and other incontinence. *Just hold it together*, I'd tell myself every morning. I'd call in sick and we'd both collapse on our beds and sleep until noon. By lunch, she'd have forgotten her hours of dark insomnia. By lunch, the nightmare was mine all alone.

And that is how we'll still be years from now.

~~~

THE SUPPORT group met for just one hour twice a month. Two hours out of the roughly 720 hours in a month. There was never enough time for our long list of questions. We sat in a circle, consumed all the cookies, and took turns with our stories.

Judy, how do you know when you need more help? Like when you might have to move your mother into a facility? I asked.

The circle was quiet. By now, we all saw the gorilla in the middle of our own personal ballgame waving at us. Mugging at us.

You'll know it's time when you can't do it anymore, Judy said.

That's a tall order for a Do or Die wood element person who also happens to be a Sink or Swim daughter.

I thought Judy could give me an assessment tool and protocol of some kind that would reveal my next best steps to take. I thought the doctors or nurses would warn me at some point—flag me down and help me surrender.

If not, I thought maybe my mother's slow-motion decline would speed up and she'd die swiftly one night right before dawn and spare us all the next parts of the sequence. Or maybe she'd have a survivable stroke and a social worker in the hospital would sit me in a windowless office, offer me tea, and go over my one or two options.

I hung on for another year. I hired someone to stay overnight Monday through Friday so I could get enough sleep before going to work. But then the sitter burned out and my rental was too expensive, and I had to find both of us other places to live. I moved my mother to an assisted living facility, which came with an episode of bedbugs, a nurse's aide who twisted my mother's arm, a fall that cut her arm from elbow to wrist, and a couple of trips to the ER. Finally, she required a skilled nursing facility, which I visited every day after work or during work or instead of work. After nine months, she qualified for a Medicaid bed in the same nursing facility. The day after Thanksgiving, my eighty-pound mother was moved to the Medicaid bed in a different room on a different wing with different nurses. It didn't take much to throw her off balance. She cried and looked lost after the move to her new room. Her arms sprawled over the sides of her carriage. Her eyes looked like blue stars dying in space.

What happened was my sympathetic nerves came down with shingles that rattled the nerves on the left side of my face, neck, and shoulder. Her crying, or my crying, would set off the tangle of electrified glass that seemed lodged just under my skin. I blinked back the glass and sang songs to my mother—*All is calm, all is bright.*

I took out her teeth and I helped her lie down. I stroked her hair and her cheeks and in four days she was gone.

I blinked back more glass and cleaned out her things from the room where she died in her Medicaid bed. I collected her ashes from the Cremation Society of North Carolina and carried them to the beach two days before Christmas.

This is a love story that scatters me around.

Part 12

There is a sacredness in tears.

—WASHINGTON IRVING

THE MORNING AFTER SHE DIED, I could feel my mother's relief, as though she were dancing on the yellow shores of a lake light years away. I waited to feel my own lake of relief. I waited to feel a river of grief, but all I felt was a world of fatigue.

The morning after, I stood numb in my kitchen.

I boiled a kettle of water and drank a cup of mint tea without sitting down. I thought I heard someone tap at my door. No one ever tapped at my door unless I knew they were coming or it was a mistake of some kind. No one was there when I looked through the peephole. I opened the door and a big calico cat slipped inside and rubbed around my shins. She must've been a neighbor's cat. She wasn't a stray, and she wasn't a wolf.

Only females can have three colors in their fur. I learned this after Napper surprised us with the first litter of kittens. *See her three colors?* a friend of my mother's asked me. *See her orange, black, and tan? That makes her a tortoiseshell and that means she's a female.*

If this were a dream, I wondered, what would an unexpected calico cat visitor mean? Later, I would read that tricolored cats mean good luck in Japan.

She sat on my couch and watched me move around my place. She had a look on her face that went with the thought—*You are not alone.* I had a look on my face that went with the thought—*I'm so glad you are here.*

I sat down on the couch as luck purred alongside me. A few heavy tears rolled over my shingles. I let the cat stay all morning long, like when a package is delivered to my place by mistake. The calico napped on my couch. She meowed at the front door after lunch, and I let her out to let her go home.

A few weeks after, I had to have a molar extracted. The dentist rocked my roots back and forth while all of my teeth felt the big storm. At the end, one tree fell out of my mouth. The dentist packed up the hole with gauze and showed me the molar with its main root infected. My face was numb and confused for the rest of the day. The forest took weeks to get over the place where my tooth used to be.

I lay on my couch for three days in a row, spent from the month of shingles and now missing a molar. I tracked the days' passing in angles of yellow that slid up and down my living room world. Then the sunlight turned orange and fell off the wall. Where was my mother now that she wasn't a lady and wasn't a tiger?

I looked around at the things I'd inherited from her—the slim Danish desk, the George Dureau still-life painting he gave my mother before he was New Orleans famous, the shelf of books, and her wire-rim bifocals. I'd learned long ago how to sit with what's absent until presence appears. These childhood friends surrounded me now. Our bonds strong as ever and our roots intertwined. I found my mother the way I'd always found her—in all the things she left behind.

~~

YOU HAVE *nothing left*, the acupuncturist said. She held my wrist and felt my pulse as I lay flat on my back on her treatment table. *Your well is bone dry.*

I know, I told her. *I feel like the desert.* Then my very last drops spilled down my cheeks. I closed my eyes while she needled the sensitive points.

She patted my shoulder in between the long needles. *Caregiving takes a toll.*
  I nodded.
  You're like the lamp, the plug, and the outlet all in one, she said.
  Better than no light, I said.

She walked around the table and felt the qi in the pulse of my other dry wrist. I felt the room's fern-green walls and the Asian decor. I felt the cool of her fingertips feeling for me. I felt my pulse echo back from the base of my well.

The emotional body has a mind of its own, she said. *Remember to breathe through the soles of your feet. Exhale like a flashlight, not like a candle.*

She moved around the room like a willow. She turned down the lights and turned on the ocean with flutes and drumbeats and a high lonesome note.

Visualize roots as much as you can. We want you to come down to the planet for a change and live here with us.

I've lived most of my life on the top floors of buildings. I've grown tomatoes on fire escapes in black plastic bags. My roots seem to be wedded to the emergency exit.

It didn't occur to me that it wouldn't occur to her that I wasn't the one who flew away from the world. The world is the one that packed up and left me.

I closed my eyes. I swallowed my tears and slept like a desert.

No less than the trees and the stars . . .

DON'T BE *scared*, I would tell my mother during her days of dementia. *I'm not going to leave you.*

I know, she would say without looking at me.

How do you know? I wanted to ask. But that wasn't her worry; that wasn't her nightmare. She was fine in the dark. The panic was mine.

B. F. Skinner wrote about how the mind works. How we are more likely to fill in the gaps and see completed circles and squares when confronted with incomplete shapes. Of course, the same phenomenon applies when the shape is a parent.

When my mother was still alive and before I turned thirty, I went to see a psychic who lived in a high-rise in midtown Manhattan. There was no incense or gris-gris or candles on the table. Just a small living room up in the air with a picture glass window full of skyscrapers. We sat on her white leather couch. A long-haired gray cat was curled up between us. The cat and I were more voodoo than she was, but I warmed to her wavelength full of strong buildings.

In numerology, thirty is busy. Thirty is an optimist with the auspicious number three followed by the magic of zero. Thirty is ready to build a future that's brighter.

I've lived in New York City for ten years now, but I don't feel like I fit. Should I stay or should I move? What do you think of North Carolina?

The psychic saw my stomachaches and insomnia. She saw into my past.

No matter where you live, it's time to consider expelling your old secrets. Then your stomach might just settle down.

I flew back home for a week and walked around New Orleans rehearsing what I'd say to my mother.

I visited the Sun Shop on Maple Street—a shop full of art the owner bought from tribes strewn across the South and Southwest. I had enough turquoise. I needed fresh luck for the talk with my mother. I settled on a small piece of wood carved into the shape of a shack in the side of a cliff. The shack had a good vibe with a slanted roof and an arched doorway with a decorative window. Not bad for a shack. I pretended a big-hearted big sister lived in the shack and was full of big sister protection for me. Someone who could feel me, like the psychic in midtown who made feeling me seem easy. Even with the shack and an imaginary sister I still shuddered at the idea of telling my secret.

My mother and I sat down in her kitchen. She had a bowl of rice in her hands and a glass of red wine on the table. I told her my story. The tiny shack of fresh luck that I held in my palms trembled and shook. The old earth cracked open, and my mother stopped eating. She slammed her bowl on the table. Rice scattered around us like a ceremonial offering to appease angry gods.

Why are you telling me this? She was hot; she was mad. She walked like a gun as she walked out of the room.

We wrote letters to each other after I left and moved to North Carolina. Letters I saved where she moved from mad to sad feelings. Letters where I coached her through all the trouble. Who better to help her recover than me?

The natal moon reflects one's emotional system and the place of the mother.

My moon is in Cancer trapped in the eighth house of exiles and secrets.

I find the moon almost every night somewhere in the sea of sky or shimmering in a pool of water. She always slips away of course, yellow-wasted on the bluesy earth, complicated through the trees' complicated tangles.

JAYCEE DUGARD was abducted at the age of eleven and held in a backyard compound of tents and sheds for eighteen long years. At night, she'd look up at the moon outside of her tent. She'd imagine her mother at home looking up at the moon at the very same time.

I sat with hundreds of other court employees from all over the country in an auditorium in Washington, DC. We were gathered at a conference on trauma-informed court practices. Jaycee stood small on the stage behind a stout wooden podium and described the ways intuition had saved her again and again. During captivity, she cultivated what some call *soldier's intuition* and some call *women's intuition*—the sixth sense needed to navigate minefields of all kinds.

Jaycee told us that she never once forgot that the man was her captor, but she did learn to watch him and read him from inside her confinement. She was predator and prey. *Mostly prey*, she told us.

Two women security officers at the University of California in Berkeley trusted their gut feelings when Jaycee's abductor walked onto campus with his two children. He wanted to lecture the university students about the virtues of Christianity. Instead of turning him away, the officers trusted what they called their *mother's intuition*. This is how Jaycee's abduction finally came to an end. Now she talks with police officers and court officials about the importance of caring and feeling your feelings.

Toward the end of her talk, Jaycee apologized for not having saved herself or the kids she'd had while in captivity. I could feel her feeling that somehow she'd contributed to the whole awful mess. Afterward, I went up to meet her. We held hands for a minute and looked at each other. I told her she did—save herself—she wasn't a traitor.

⁓⁓

I NEEDED to find a few more coins to fill up my red bank before the year ended. On the sidewalk in front of a grocery store, something silver caught my eye. Maybe a dime? It looked like a bead.

I bent down and saw a tiny Buddha tumbled upside down on the pavement. I thought of the Tibetan man in New York City, the pennies he picked up and the Buddha statue on his stoop. I thought of Caine in China and the Buddhas all around him. The tiny silver Buddha was smaller than a penny, half the size of my thumbnail. I put him in the palm of my hand. He sat there balanced in the pose of a lotus.

Synchronicity means *the coincidental occurrence of events that seem related but are not explained by conventional causality.*

In physics and electricity, synchronicity means *having the same frequency* and *zero phase difference.*

⁓⁓

SUR·VIVE sər-ˈvīv/
verb
    1. continue to live or exist after an event, especially in spite of danger or hardship.
Example in a sentence—*against all odds the child survived.*
Synonyms of **survive**—*to pull through, keep body and soul together.*

My mother's obituary listed me as one of her survivors. All I had to do was to continue to exist in spite of her absence. I was already an expert at this kind of surviving.

In the Wim Wenders film *Wings of Desire*, the angels lived mostly in public libraries. Maybe they liked settings where people gathered freely to learn and to lend to one another. The angels in the libraries had both kinds of superpowers—flight and invisibility. Some wanted to renounce their gifts, come down to earth, and live here like us—exposed and on foot.

There is no section in my neighborhood library dedicated to true stories of survival, the lost-in-the-woods-and-made-it-out-alive kind of stories. Or the kind of true story in *She Left Me the Gun*, where the author, Emma Brockes, wrote about how she discovered her mother's secret life of childhood sexual assault at the hands of her mother's father. And how this trauma secretly informed Emma's whole life.

Survivors' stories are scattered everywhere—the memoir section, the outdoor adventure section, the history section, and all through the current events, like a network or roots you could walk across on.

Dear Emma Brockes,
    Thank you for telling your story in She Left Me the Gun. *Our secrets are screaming and still it's so hard to share them.*

Emma wrote back. *Yes it is, but the sky won't fall down.*

I stopped by the checkout desk at the library. *Why do you think there's no survival story section?* I asked.
    The librarian cocked her head to the side for a second. *Not enough interest, I guess.*

Less than 1 percent of reported rapes result in a felony conviction. Nearly all survivors of sexual violence must manage the physical and mental aftereffects of trauma.

As I headed for the door, I knew I passed at least a half dozen survivors who kept their heads down and, like me, blended in with the rest of the stories.

When I got home, I looked online for more true-life stories of survival. I found an old interview with a woman named Tere who survived all alone for four days at sea when she was eleven years old. The captain of the yacht her parents had hired murdered her entire family. Then he scuttled the boat and escaped on a dinghy. Tired from stabbing people, he'd bet on the little girl he'd initially overlooked going down with the wreckage. But the girl found a small cork float in the dark as the boat sank beneath her. She sat on the float for four days in the ocean, and then she was rescued. If a storm had overtaken her on the float or if she'd just fallen asleep and fallen off the cork float, Tere and her story and her body and soul would not have pulled through to continue together.

Oh, *this* is what it is to survive—you find what floats and then you hold on. Even if what floats is smaller than you.

After the rescue and after the hospital, Tere was sent to live with relatives in Wisconsin. Those relatives thought it would be better if she never mentioned the story again. *Pretend it's not there.* She grew up and changed her name from Terry Jo to Tere. Later in life, maybe after those relatives grew old with dementia and then passed away, Tere found other survivors to talk with. She saw what she couldn't see clearly before. She started telling her story, and the sky didn't fall down.

In the article, the interviewer asked Tere why she chose to work in a water resources department and live by a lake. The interviewer was baffled by her choice. He imagined that Tere would be afraid of bodies of water and would avoid them at all costs. Wouldn't the water trigger the memories of the events she had lived through?

Tere explained that the opposite was true. She developed a bond with the water after four days on a cork float. I imagined Tere's difficulty explaining to the interviewer the roots that you develop when you are floating all alone. The ocean didn't stab her family to death and scuttle the ship. The ocean was just doing what oceans do.

I imagined the interviewer would then turn to me and ask—*And what was your ocean?*

I imagined my answer—*Solitude.*

Part 13

One minute I was a princess, the next I was a witch.

—NATASCHA KAMPUSCH

THE AVERAGE AMERICAN MOVES eleven and a half times in their lifetime. If your roots were never that deep to begin with, the count is much higher. I'm on the edge of thirty-nine. My landlord's given me a year to find out where I belong. He's ready to cash in on his condo now that downtown is booming. I can't say that I blame him—I'd do the same thing if I walked like a landlord instead of a state employee nearing retirement.

It's easy to scoot around Raleigh and scope out places to live now that my mother has passed on. But each open house I attend is a trigger. On the outside the condos are gray or blasé and look like they don't belong anywhere. They stare off into space, like hotels dissociating on the side of the highway. I feel stranded and cold with aluminum siding, and inside's no better.

If it weren't for the hurricanes and the flying cockroaches, I'd move back to New Orleans and live alongside Katrina survivors. If it weren't for my job and the odds stacked against finding another job at this point in life, I'd move back anyway. It's where I belong, or at least that's what I think from my rental in Raleigh.

Everywhere you go, there you are—says my young neighbor when I tell her the news that I'll be moving on once I find where I fit. She's heading off to play tennis, bouncing a ball on her racket without looking.

She's the same neighbor who handed me a hardback story she'd finished reading one day when I came home from work. The story of a young woman who grew up in the midst of her father's end-times worldview due to his untreated bipolar disorder. The author wrote of her struggles to leave her family and heal up her past.

I am pretty sure I would have left that family long before she did, my neighbor had told me.

I sucked my teeth and looked away to the trees.

~~~

I TAKE a light-blue marble from my collection of marbles and found objects I keep in an ashtray in my kitchen. I drop the marble into a small hole on the sidewalk by the one townhouse I like. This townhouse sits just one block from the condo where I no longer belong and has windows that smile onto a small park. I could live in this townhouse if someone would sell it, and if I had a boatload of cold cash instead of blue marbles.

The *New York Times* has a free "Rent or Buy" calculator for use on its website because, as it turns out, this is a popular question. But my math isn't helping. The calculator analyzes my data, and my score is dead even.

I pull the large Random House dictionary onto my lap, the dictionary my mother brought with her to my place after the storm. The binding is frayed, and inside, a few torn pages have been taped back together. I flip the dictionary pages back and forth, eyes closed, and feel for a word to help with my rent-or-buy question. My finger lands on a word. I look down at the page and I find the word *knife-edge*.

I shut the dictionary. Everywhere I go, a knife-edge seems to follow. After a few minutes, I go back and read the knife-edge's definition—*an uncertain situation, a challenging balance.*

We are all *migratory beings.* I've just migrated more than the average migrator. I've moved around and around, but there are so many ways I've never moved in.

Maybe I just need to lighten up more. I lug boxes of books out of my condo and drive them to the local used bookstore. I heave them into the collection bin and listen as they thud their goodbye. I cull the clothes from the back of my closet that never wanted to stay in the first place. I pack them off to Goodwill along with a stack of plates and a fistful of spoons that are unemployed with just their one diner.

I go through the single condo closet that still holds my mother. These things can go now—a bag of yellow yarn she bought on sale before Katrina, her collection of old sketch pads, boxes of colored pencils still sharp and unused, the random pages of old love letters she clung to like lifejackets. But I will keep the journal she wrote the year I was born—the dark place she inhabited, the gut feeling she had that my father would soon leave us. There was no space to mention a new baby in there. She told me once that I slept so much that first year she thought I was dying. *Should I stay or should I go?*

I'll also keep my mother's booklet of postcards with Paul Klee's artwork on the front side of each card. I'll put these cards in the kitchen cabinets of my next residence and wherever I go I will surprise myself when I reach for a white bowl and see *Fish Magic* and *Flower Myth* leaning against a stack of new moons.

I flip to the back of the postcard book and read a Klee quote. *Art does not reproduce the visible; rather, it makes visible.* The way overlooked pink stars and marbles come alive when they're noticed.

~~~

WHERE SHOULD I move, closer to the end now at sixty years old? I can go anywhere, so I go back to New Orleans, my home all along, on a two-week vacation. What would it be like to live where I started? I fit better on streets that sag, where live oaks lay low, and rain falls in sheets all afternoon. I stay in a shotgun house again, where one poor room is just like another.

There's a quote from Pema Chodron on my calendar for the month of May—*Usually, we think that brave people have no fear. The truth is that they are intimate with fear.*

The truth is I am close to alone.

Superman said the cure for loneliness is solitude. The Buddha said the cure for sadness is joy. Leonard Cohen said there is no cure for love. The task is to stand on the teeter-totter with a foot on each side and balance.

All through the middle, I've stayed in touch with my English teacher from high school. Her son has a house in the New Orleans Mid-City area. A house he Airbnbs to me for two weeks at a discounted rate for *friends of the family*. I am no longer a friend with a mother uptown by the river—not since she and Katrina both passed.

I've been homesick forever because there's no place like home. Just déjà vu.

The Airbnb is half a mile from City Park and the St. Louis Cemetery No. 3. Tour buses stop there to show off the way we've stacked graves above ground, above our below-sea-level ground so the dead don't float off. When your roots are in water, it's tempting to float off.

When I lie in bed in my Airbnb, I feel ten friends from here—mostly gone. Mostly dope. They follow me to the sink like prayers. I cup my hands underwater and wash my face, dress up my past, be here for now. I could keep on going and adopt every state, take on new names—Hope, Mercy, maybe Shame, maybe Eleven. The ten would ride along with me and sing our songs. I'll stay put for now and write it out in short-form poems. I'll take long walks, feed stray cats and dogs, my little not-disappearing acts.

How I Made Good. How I Live Now after What I Lived Through. I've come back home to bring it all forward. I'll use everything, like the woman who'd been homeless before she'd been to Harvard. Like her answer during a radio show when the interviewer asked her how she made good after what she'd lived through. *I don't waste anything. I use it all, even sadness, even anger.* The interviewer went silent.

Some 70 percent of sexual assaults stay unreported. How many of those survive all the way? How many of the ten were 70 percent? Our roots were in water and then theirs were gone.

~~~

THERE'S NO *art in trusting no one.* That's what the burned-out spy told the young wannabe spy in the movie I watched on Netflix last night. *The art of the spy is to find the right one—the one you can trust.*

I don't remember the spies' names or their missions or any of their spy secrets. I only remember how the burned-out spy, the best of the lot, wore a tie every day and read books in the evening with his gray tabby cat asleep on his lap. He was ready to retire after years of harassment from the heterosexual spies in the rest of the department. The young spy was skittish, suicidal sometimes, empathic most times. He wore the same clothes scene after scene as he struggled to find the right people to trust. Like all skittish survivors, his antenna was sharp and flooded with feelings that were rarely his own. The art of the spy can be very messy.

The days in New Orleans bend with slow-motion heat. The sky is fat with clouds the color of concrete. Nothing above is moved by our sweltering condition below on the ground. I go back in time with every memory humid and close. *We're socked in,* my mother used to say when a weather front pressed down on us like a sinus infection.

A loose dog lies under the house. Chickens and cats are under the shotgun next door. I forgot how many strays live in New Orleans. Our Blessed Mother guards the yard—her flooded past, our humid eyes. One poor girl is just like another. We fall in sheets all afternoon.

I'm socked in now, a few feet below sea level with my past infected. The unflappable part was always a cover.

I brought a backpack of books, but mostly I read and reread Maggie Nelson's tiny *Bluets*. I am in love with how she's in love with blue. I'm in love with how she writes it out in little paragraphs just like me. Am I kin to her? Am I channeling her? Am I friends with her?

Maggie breathes blue. I inhale green and exhale Spanish moss. My mother smoked white sailboats on a menthol-green lake. She leaned forward with a Salem—always somewhere better to go.

In third grade, I learned that Salem was more than a brand of cigarettes. I learned how women on trial were thrown into lakes with rocks tied around them. The guilty floated and then they were burned. The drowned all went free. I'm just as guilty as the undrowned, nowhere better to go.

I open the door and call for the loose dog who needs a good name— *Ginger* is good. She crawls out from under the house when I call. I love her rust-colored coat marbled with gray, and she loves me color-blind. She inhales my scent and I exhale the house. This is what it's like to love the undrowned. We share what we've found. We use everything.

I give her a bowl full of water and a saucer of peanut butter. She can't believe her good luck. She gives me almond eyes and her wide pink smile. I see scabs on her legs and fleas in her ears and I wonder if she'll let me give her a bath or if she'll growl and run off. Ginger finishes her peanut butter and trots off down the sidewalk. Sometimes it's impossible to know who to trust. Sometimes relief comes when you just run away and keep your skittish self safe, even when your self is bitten and bleeding.

Liuzza's on Bienville Street has been serving local food since before I was born. Though I'm not much of a foodie, my favorite is the shrimp po-boy special. Photos of Liuzza hang on the peach-colored walls like family portraits—Liuzza up to her awning in Katrina's dark floodwater, Liuzza during the years of repair, Liuzza celebrating her restoration after the storm with a full house of customers. I look around at everyone now busy with lunch, and they all bear a Katrina resemblance.

Restaurants and churches and shops around the city have plaques high on their walls. The plaques honor the flood's waterline they somehow survived. The resilient understand this *before* and *after* teeter-totter and the need to mark both sides of the story somehow. A version of strength is drawn from tattoos and old scars and plaques on the wall.

The *after* follows you forward on the crest of a wave. The *before* gets smaller like a city you fly out of on a red-eye one night. You can't can't look down at the fierce lights below—that place where you come from. That place you could block out with the palm of your hand flat on the window. That place that would actually swallow you whole if you went back and landed.

~~~

BUDDY WAS a twenty-something Vietnam vet when I was a teenager. We used to get high together in Audubon Park. He inhaled dark gray and exhaled a war. When his blue eyes went bloodshot, he'd show us his scars and the lump of shrapnel still in his shoulder just under the skin. Another small piece had been removed from his cheek. Any higher and he would have been blind. Any deeper and he would have been dead. There were so many ways he had almost been dead. He'd had a hole drilled through that ugly twist of souvenir shrapnel so he could slip a silver chain through and wear it around his neck. The same silver chain held one small Jesus in a crooked pose on the cross. Whenever Buddy moved fast or took off his shirt, his two amulets jangled their stories in the air all around him.

What almost takes you out can become your companion—if you carry it out of the war zone and tend to it better.

In the early twentieth century, English-speaking psychologists wanted their own version of the German psychological term *Einfühlung*, literally meaning *feeling-in*. Two psychologists from Cornell and Cambridge suggested *empathy* from the Greek *empathei*, literally meaning *in-feeling*.

Empath, taken as an agent noun, was first known to be used in 1956. But even before 1956, the good spies have always been empaths.

I don't know where Buddy is now. I can't really feel him feeling alive, but I hope he's come forward, carrying a small Jesus, stacking one day on top of the other. I hope he didn't just float away and finish off what the war left inside him.

~~~

I HAVE qi stuck in my throat. It feels like a plum pit and like I might vomit. My acupuncturist thinks the cause is liver disharmony and energy stagnation. I think the cause is the words that I'm writing now without skimming over. Could be the same thing.

Not telling isn't always a decision . . .

but telling is.

Now that we have terms like PTSD and adverse childhood experiences, I decide to tell my story to my family physician—for the sake of my stomach, which she's trying to heal. It's been ages since I've told anyone any part of this story.

I can't tell what she thinks as she sits there and takes notes. I've listened to peers, unaware of my story, describe how they're so feisty and fierce, no one could snatch them without a bazooka. Is this what she'll say to her friends after work? She palpates my stomach, then gives me the name of a licensed nutritionist.

Now my story sits in my medical portal—*kidnapped and raped at fourteen years old.*

Is it the story that marks me or the telling that does it?

My quietude and stillness are a home that I've built, and there's no place like home. I walk around town—my haunts are torn down. I walk old on new streets like a ghost passing through. I lean my back against the trees still here, thick-skinned and fat with years.

~~~

I WAS a pretty good little spy in elementary school. I could feel who were the tyrants and who were their minions in every new school in every new year. In third grade, in Arabi, just east of New Orleans, my antenna said *ally* when I crossed paths with Pee Wee. No one much liked him and no one liked me. Because he lived with his family by the levee in a tumbledown shack and I lived in an apartment without any father. Because he couldn't read and I couldn't write cursive. Because I wished I were a boy so I could wear pants to school and play marbles at recess. Because Pee Wee put a towel over his crew cut at night and wished he were a girl prized for his kindness and his honey long hair. We trusted each other with our third-grade secrets. In a year, my mother moved us again and I lost Pee Wee forever.

Sympathy came first. Then Empathy. Then Empath.

I don't know if Pee Wee survived long into adulthood, but the chances aren't good. I'd heard a rumor once that he'd died young, stuck in Angola—our state penitentiary. Still, I'd like to think that he made it somehow and if I'd stayed put in Arabi we'd have looked out for each other. Two spies are better than one sleeper agent left on their own.

I may not have a circle of people around me, but I can feel where they'd fit. I can feel Pee Wee close by.

I drive the six miles over to Arabi on the other side of the Lower Ninth Ward, down Friscoville Avenue, past the elementary school. Little has changed in the area since my year in third grade. The apartment is there along with the corner store full of candy and the bar by the levee. I get out of my car and see that Pee Wee's shack is all gone. I walk around the block missing Pee Wee. Half a dozen trailers sit there instead, aging in place. Weeds up to my waist.

Pee Wee was called Pee Wee because he stayed smaller than his older brothers and the other Arabi boys with their muscular jaws and their long string-bean bodies who practiced spitting and throwing firecrackers at cars that drove by. Who talked about fucking and who dared one another to fuck one of the animals in the stable by the levee. They swore they'd seen men strap the hind legs of sheep into their work boots to keep the sheep still. The dark shock of these stories made me feel like a creature they might strap down next. I stayed close to Pee Wee and we stayed to ourselves.

Turns out the stable in Arabi was more of a small stockyard and the stockyard was a remnant of the old slaughterhouse system. Arabi had slaughtered meat for the fancy in New Orleans since by law New Orleans had to keep its own fancy slaughter-free. The stench and the blood were left for those on the outskirts, those in the margins. There's always a work-around, a cutout, a loophole to be found when dark money's involved. You can still feel the dirty deal when you walk around Arabi. Old blood traps in backyards. Boys roaming the levee.

~~

I TAKE a walk in the morning before it's too hot. I walk through City Park under the arms of live oak trees where it's good and dark green. The New Orleans Museum of Art sits in the front of the park. I walk up the steps into air-conditioned rooms full of paintings that look like half-remembered half dreams.

The description on the wall next to the section of "Self-Taught Artists" uses words like *raw* and *unfiltered*. The self-taught use whatever the day's synchronicity has put in their path—bottle caps, rubber bands, dropped earrings, old pencils.

I stop by Liuzza's for a take-home order of red beans and rice. Then I walk home through the raw heat of midday. I see Ginger's rust-colored shape in the dark gap under the house. I leave half the red beans and rice lunch on a paper plate by the steps. She comes out to eat right away and she practically sings. She tells me she takes nothing for granted—I'm no pet whisperer, but it's all over her eyes. Nothing in her expression or her aura includes a life with a person looking out for her welfare. No shared meals on patios with lights strung overhead. No owner who sings songs about first loves by the lakeside. Not that she begrudges anyone these things. Not that she believes in any of these things.

~~~

WHEN I first read about the Great Sparrow Campaign, I thought it said the Great Sorrow Campaign. In China, in 1958, Chairman Mao wanted the small birds dead. He claimed the sparrows were pests who damaged the crops. Three million citizens were commanded to blanket the countryside. They banged pots and made constant noise so the sparrows had nowhere to rest, nowhere to land that was safe. After days of this, the dead fell from the sky. Other sparrows crash-landed in exhaustion and were then stomped dead by soldiers and children.

The Polish embassy in Beijing refused to participate in the sorrow. For a while, their grounds became a quiet green refuge full of hushed birds. I imagine Polish diplomats scattering bread crumbs and setting out bowls of fresh water for their asylum seekers who huddled in the trees. But soon the drummers surrounded the property and beat on and on for days and on and on until these birds too, fell from their hiding and fell to the ground. Everywhere the undrowned learn to live small. Even then, the odds are against us.

Why have you stayed silent for so long?

When I tell the part of my story where I stayed alive, where I lived through my nightmare, what I'm also telling is that I went to hell first with a man in his truck who thanked me that night for being on his side. And I played along the way an animal plays dead. *It's a nice night. I'll walk.* And everywhere I go—rent or buy, stay or move, fly away or be seen—I've been to hell first. I've been on his side.

It's a dirty shame.

The campaign was deemed a success. The sparrows were almost disappeared across all the country. But then the sparrows weren't there to eat up the bugs that ate up the crops, and especially the locusts that ate on and on. Historians today think this Great Campaign was a major cause of the Great Famine that took over 50 million human lives.

The species of sparrows defied the odds and returned to China years and years later. Now it's the story of the campaign that's gone missing. Journalist Yang Jisheng documents the Great Sparrow Campaign in his work *Tombstone*. The book's been banned in China, disappeared as a pest. Is it the story that marks us or the telling that does it?

Our history is all fabricated. It's been covered up, he said. *If a country can't face its own history, then it has no future.*

In other words, bring the story forward—where we can be better. Where we can better tend to the arc and the allegory this time around. Where those exiled as traitors can describe the forbidden.

Dear Mr. Brave Jisheng Journalist,
How lucky we are not to have the mind of a chairman. How lucky we are to be the kind to salvage missing stories from the past for the sake of our future.

If I get another tattoo, it will be of a sparrow safe on my left shoulder, my yin shoulder, the embassy of compassion. And whenever someone asks about my sparrow tattoo, I will tell the story of how the beaten-down birds slowly came home on the crest of a wave.

～～～

I HAVE a few detached relatives I never see anymore. There are a few friends here and there, and we talk through the distance to keep a small fire lit. I stay warm enough.

Whenever I'm in New Orleans, I think of looking for Gifford. I miss him. I hate him. It's too much to balance. Everywhere you go, there's one knife-edge or another.

I shower off the New Orleans heat at the end of a sweaty day—the best part of a long sweaty day. My aura holds a strong scent of soap with hints of sandalwood and mint. I sit on the front steps and watch as the spent sun lowers into the gray haze of treetops. The houses relax their hot clapboard glare. The headache of parked cars cools down like pools of water. A neighbor walks by and nods. I nod back at her and for a moment we look lucky slanted in old sunlight.

～～～

SLEEP IS *my friend*, I tell myself. I don't believe myself. Not when it's dark and there's no place like home. I need more friends. What I have is Joni Mitchell songs stuck in my head. *I really don't know love at all.*

I know it's late. The electric clock is a cold box that glows in the corner—triggered and ticking. Rectangles of window light slant across the wall over the foot of my bed like edgy art. The whole room is a canvas in the middle of the night. Black and white is the medium and the only interpretation. I try to visualize a pink-yellow sunrise to wash all the Dada away. What I get is acid reflux and a minor gray headache.

I sit up and stare at the wall without blinking—trying to exhaust my wide-awake eyes, trying to trick them into feeling sleepy. My eyes just feel dry. I blink hard several times. I kind of yawn, a puny yawn, a kitten yawn. A kitten that won't go to sleep.

If a black dog is evocative of clinical depression, is a wide-awake kitten the same for insomnia? Or is this just my thyroid swinging hyper again, spilling over with thoughts I'd rather not follow? I've been here before with this very same kitten.

I lie back down and make shapes with my body under the covers as though I am falling from a plane in the air. A fetus, a windmill, a steak knife—which shape best survives a long-distance drop? The *New York Times* said a fetus because survivors fall small. Like an ant, they said, that falls out of tree. Mostly the ant will get up and walk away. A person mostly will not. But I know the advantage any ant has when it falls from a tree is its shiny black armor. The article failed to mention this pertinent fact.

My third-grade teacher taught us science once a week. She'd stand by the sink in the back of the classroom because science can get messy. Once she held up a dead beetle the size of a pickle pinned to a white cardboard square. *Tock tock* she tapped on the back of the beetle with the tip of her nail.

Exoskeleton, she said. *The opposite of us. Our bones are on the inside. Our softness is on the outside.*

Like decorations? I asked her. *Like a Christmas tree?*

In the morning, I wake up like a clock. A helicopter's overhead, beating the air. But this is not 'Nam, not Afghanistan. The radio reports cops up above. A man dumped a woman out of his truck onto the avenue that feeds the heart of the city. Or else she jumped to escape the not 'Nam-Afghanistan war in that truck. The man fled on foot when the chopper hovered over his Chevy Silverado speeding north of the city. All day he's at large, like a storm in the sky. All day she's out cold in a ward on a wing. I feel all small how she jumped or was dumped in the shape of a log that rolled across the road that feeds the heart of the city.

WHEN WE say the word *algebra*, we are saying the *reunion of broken parts* in Arabic.

Muḥammed ibn Mūsā al-Khwārizmī, who started the algebra revolution, who wrote *The Book of Restoration and Balancing*, turned universities upside down and better with his revolutionary way of solving problems.

One translator twisted al-Khwārizmī's name and referred to him as Algoritmi instead. Over time, this pronunciation further warped and became *Algorithm*.

Whenever we say *algorithm*, we are really saying *al-Khwārizmī*. Some stories follow us forward in disguise and we never know it.

I fly back to Raleigh and play hooky from work for a couple more days while I try to decide where I'll move next. I float flat on my back in the condo pool in the middle of the summer weekday. I have the pool to myself. My arms go wide in water. Two dots above me, specks in blue sky, like freckles or floaters, are barely there. I see sunlight flash silver on one of the specks and make out its wings. I float below the pair as they dip and dodge and float together in midair play.

Should I rent or should I buy?

This is what I ask a psychic empath during a telephone call with boxes half full on the floor all around me. *I have to do something soon*, I tell her.

I found this empath on YouTube, where she channels good news. *Trump won't last long. We have to stay calm*—she's been telling us for months while sitting in front of her California window with sun pouring in.

I imagine her at her desk and the window behind her while we talk on the phone. She channels the West Coast to me on the East.

Or should I move back to New Orleans and live there again? It's just me on my own with this decision to make.

I hear her take a couple of deep breaths and whisper a prayer for invisible protection. Then she interrupts her own prayer with a gasp.

What? I ask.

She tells me that something from my past has shown up in this reading. She hesitates. Then she asks if someone tried to hurt me when I was a kid.

He killed a few other girls, she says. *Looks like he got caught and went to prison somewhere.*

I hold my breath. Why does my history show up in my future?

The bones of one's story always show up in a reading.

Like an X-ray? I ask her.

Yes, like an X-ray, she says.

What she sees on my X-ray is me at fourteen. She describes all the fractures.

The girls he killed couldn't stop crying. It pissed him off. They panicked and he killed them. Somehow you settled him down. Does this make sense? she asks me.

Makes sense, I tell her. I was groomed to not panic.

As for my rent-or-buy question and the thoughts I was entertaining of moving back home, she doesn't really answer. *You'll always be a bit unsure of your shelter. Moving in makes you nervous. But you're OK, you're OK.*

Before the call ends, she tells me that two is my number.

In numerology. That's your life shape number—a two. Twos are good at partnering with others. You should be living communally or something. Don't stay in the margins! She sounds almost worried. *This event has affected your life number. The job of a two is to show up for other people.*

I tell her how I show up for other people when I mediate their conflicts. Because their war isn't mine, their peace isn't either. I stay limber like a contortionist and fit where I'm needed. Sounds like a zero, but it could be two.

~~~

YOU SHOULD *downsize,* a colleague tells me. She's come into my office as I scroll through a website of condos for sale. *Live in a studio or rent an RV, but definitely downsize and think about moving closer to family.*

Because she's sixty like me but has a big house and family and can't see how downsized my life already is.

I'm the opposite of you. I'm a spy, a spook, and now I'm trying to show up for myself and finish my story.

I don't say any of this out loud in the room of course. I know when to keep quiet and not blow my cover.

~~~

I DRIVE away from thirty-eight, my favorite residence so far, with all that I own in the back of a van. The van's large enough for my middle-age spread of a round coffee table and a midcentury bureau. What I wanted was another small condo to live in—three rooms that flow into each other and onto the balcony. This time I'd own it. But small has become chic with a homeowner's fee I would choke on each month. Instead, I drive to the outskirts of town and the affordable two-story townhouse I've bought. Its downstairs goes dark when I am upstairs in bed, but I do what I can. I leave the lights on.

I set one piece of furniture in each room in the new place.
    They look like beasts in a zoo with nothing to do.

Which room is yours? people ask me at work when I show them photos of the rooms that I've painted.
    Aren't all of them mine?

But none of the rooms are talking to me yet. They are deserted and still and unable to root. The feeling's contagious and it's a feeling I hate, so I rotate myself throughout all the rooms. I dress for work in the bedroom on the east side of the townhouse—the room with the rug. At the end of the day, I undress in the west.

Most weekends I sleep on the couch facing the front door. I charge my laptop in the bathroom, brush my teeth on the stairs. I circle around like a dog lying down.

I drive though the outskirts and take in the new landscape. I can go anywhere. A few miles down the road, I spot a small round table left by the curb with a sign taped on top. *I'm Free*, the sign says. The table looks numb and forgotten, so I get out of my car and tear off the sign.

I pull the back seats down in my compact car and lift the table inside. I'll hose it down, sand off the grime, and stain her flat wooden face. I will clean her trio of iron legs, which curve in and branch out like the stems of tall flowers. I'll paint them with left-over Agreeable Gray and name her Sabine, because that's what I do—I name things around me so I can hear what they're saying. Sabine seems like the name of an agreeable French woman who would be easy to talk with. We'd sit in her kitchen early in the morning and talk over the news.

My car is my second home, my home away from home, my mini mobile home. On my days off from work, I migrate around town with whatever I might need packed in the back. In that way, I'm free.

~~

THE EMOTIONAL Freedom Technique—EFT for short—is supposed to help with sleeplessness, pain, illness, and more. That's what the EFT website claims. Our flow of physical energy kinks up when our thought energy gets stuck. This kink can keep us awake and turn our bodies against us.

The technique to unkink has something to do with the acupuncture meridians of energy and bilateral balance. The technique disrupts the usual stories filed in the brain, deep in the delta, way undercover, that deny us our good flow. This all makes more sense when you can't fall asleep and you lie in the dark with your heart pounding loud on the left side of your cage.

The instructions: tap seven or more times with the fingertips of both hands

- on the top of the head
- above the eyebrow
- the temple
- under the eye
- under the nose
- on the chin
- at the beginning of the collarbone
- under the arm

while saying—*Even though I cannot fall asleep* (or whatever other problem the tapper is feeling) *I completely and totally accept myself.*

Circle the eyes clockwise and counterclockwise. Then close your eyes and sing a song. Open and count to five. Close your eyes and sing again.

What song? I ask myself. I don't want one that will get stuck in my head. *Keep it simple,* I tell myself.

Doe a deer, a female deer . . . ONE TWO THREE FOUR FIVE . . . Doe a deer, a female deer. I sing out loud in the black-and-white room. I laugh out loud, wide-awake, in the room. Laughing has to be good for the wide-awake kitten and my bilateral balance.

Tap tap on the side of my temple. Tap tap on my stories filed in my bones.

Even though I cannot fall asleep, even though I feel on edge, I completely and totally accept myself, I tell myself. I don't completely and totally believe myself.

You have a lot of fight-or-flight syndrome going on. That's what the psychic said on the phone when I pressed her about moving. *Can you see a good world?*

We were both quiet on the phone. I could hear her soft breath. I could feel her eyes close. I let her see into my mind for a minute without blinking.

Can you visualize a place where you feel completely safe and at peace?

I searched my mind for the place missing me. Weeds up to my waist.

Some people see a room from their childhood or a favorite vacation spot or a grandparent's home, she said.

I spied all these places in all of their minds, like a long-distance movie that wasn't my own. Like a bird flying over when it's flying away.

Extrasensory perception—ESP for short. The term, popular in the '60s and '70s, is rarely used anymore. An empath is a person with an extrasensory antenna.

There are three ways that people become empaths. Some are just born as extra-sensitive beings. Some have parents who nurture this trait. For the rest, this extra is born of a trauma. The way your sense of smell changes when you smell your own slaughter.

I used to make worlds in shoeboxes I dug out of the trash. Opposite worlds from the fight-or-flight ones. I cut out trees, hills, and flowers from *Look* magazine. I pasted them to the insides of the rectangular world. I drew bright crayon lakes and tall grassy fields on the dull cardboard ground. Pee Wee helped me make bushes from clover we brought in from outside. Together we released my handful of animals into this world. I remember two brown plastic horses I'd found in the school playground; a pale-blue bird (that was also a pin my mother gave me to wear on special occasions) with flowers on her wings and a smile on her beak; a glass mouse whose tail had broken off long ago. The animals came alive in this handcrafted world. They galloped and sang. They couldn't believe their good fortune. Pee Wee painted a face on a pebble and set it down beside the glass mouse. Some days the pebble was a turtle and some days a frog. Either way, the creature was the mouse's small friend, equally tailless and equally happy. Every morning before school, I'd open the box and move the animals out of their bush beds and down to the lake. In the afternoons, Pee Wee and I would bring the world outside to get some fresh air—just on my front steps, safe in the margins of marginalized Arabi. That was as far as we could bring anything forward.

When all else fails and I can't fall asleep, I take my blanket and pillow and sleep hard on the floor with just the rug underneath me. I hum a Joni Mitchell song. *I wish I had a river so long I would teach my feet to fly.* I feel the shape of my border. My wide-awake thoughts aren't as vast as they think. I feel here on the floor, not dark in the sky—my endoskeleton tells me so. The shape of discomfort lulls me to sleep. And like a good spy, I give my past the slip and I exhale the night.

～～

I SIT on my couch in the townhouse and reread tiny *Bluets* while feeling blue wavelengths. The townhouse still hasn't told me her name, but I finally hear a faint heartbeat that's hers humming in the kitchen. She misses the one whose smell she's tucked away in the nap of the carpet and the corners of the closet. She's fixated on the fact of my thirty-nine moves. I stand on a chair in the kitchen, taller than any of her previous residents, and I make a promise to us both to try and visualize roots.

Everything is harder at night. Maybe even if you've lived in the same house for most of your life. Colors are flat and inert in the dark while noises take over. Wolves roam around everywhere, but with *Fresh Air* on the radio I feel surrounded by people with something important to say. This habit started for me as a kid—a Dick Cavett habit on the Sony TV and me milling around to the sound of intelligent questions and attentive replies. I wash my four dirty dishes and open my laptop.

My YouTube algorithm has gathered a collection of TED Talks and videos of animals being rescued from rivers and highways where people have left them to fend for themselves.

I check the electronic dead bolt I have installed on the front door. I step into the shower and leave the bathroom door open. The tinny talk from my laptop echoes inside the tumble of wet noise.

If a tree fell in the woods with no one around, would it make any sound? Spiders hear sounds through the hairs on their eight hairy legs. Certainly, the creatures living in the woods would hear the tree fall—with ears or hairs or however they hear sounds. And the beings who lived in that tree would be homeless that night. The question is faulty. The fault is to forget the worlds we don't see.

Elizabeth Smart appears on TED Talk TV. I stand still in the kitchen after my shower and listen to her as she tries not to panic.
    Do you know anyone who survives abduction?
    This was the first thing she thought when she disappeared. The live audience goes quiet. I wonder how many are thinking that what happened to Smart could never have happened to them— they're so feisty and fierce. They listen like tourists on a bus touring the Ninth Ward six months after Katrina.

The bodies of girls dumped dead in dark roadside ditches. The photos of children, the missing, the unsolved cold cases. That's what I first thought when I disappeared. Does anyone ever come back from abduction?

If you're going to rape and kill me, can't you just do it right here? Smart asked her abductor in the field by her house. That way her family would find her dead body and know what had happened to her. She hadn't run off, she wasn't missing and lost. She'd still feel their connection when she was dead in the sky.

Is she kin to me? Is she channeling me? Is she friends with me? I feel her feeling gone. The hair on my neck hears the rest of her story.

I go to sleep with a headache buried alive. The disappeared hold on to my life and worry my trees. Clouds speak their lost tongue. When the sun goes away, their eyes all shine down. There's no going back to the time before missing.

~~

ELIZABETH SMART answers the question that won't go away—
Why didn't you run? Everything we do, she tells a journalist, *we do to survive*. She was determined not to die at the hands of her captors. Now she wants to be an answer for victims who are questioned— *Why didn't you run, why didn't you fight back, why didn't you speak out sooner?*

It's easier [for the rapist] to simply dispose of the child. Once he's done with her, she's a burden. . . . They have no desire to continue listening to her complain and beg.—Michael Bourke, chief of the Behavioral Analysis Unit, US Marshals Service

Some of us stayed alive because we stayed alive small.

~~

I WAKE up with the sun. The day is the first hot day of the season, and the heat makes my headache go deep. I walk onto the small patio at the back of the townhouse and sit on the steps with my laptop. I scroll through the stories curated for me. Another missing girl case is first on my feed—this one is cold and unsolved and in California. New DNA has brought the case back to life. Linda was abducted on her way home from summer school in 1973. The girl was raped and killed, and the man is still at large. The date she was taken was the sixth of July—one day after my fifth of July date. Zoom in to the same year and add in a day. Add in a mother who was worried when her girl didn't come home. Add in the frantic search—helicopters and police dogs and lights flooding the scene from above until her young body was found in the bay. Another dead girl floating away. The latest generation of police in California have an idea to use everything and bring Linda forward—a series of tweets in the dead girl's own voice.

I've never heard of the New Orleans police force deploying an idea like this one. What I have heard of is the 800 rape kits that sat ignored and untested in the City That Care Forgot.

Phantom limb pain (PLP) is pain felt in the area in which a limb has been amputated. Nerve endings at the site of amputation send messages to the brain and trick the brain into believing that the amputated limb is still present and in pain.

Mirror therapy is for those suffering from PLP. Patients watch the reflected image of their intact limb in a mirror strategically placed where the missing limb used to be. To the patient, it appears that they can move both limbs simultaneously. Obviously, this is not true, but the patient's phantom limb relaxes, and the pain goes away.

Hi. I'm Linda. . . . Today I'm going to tell you my story.

I know this story. I lived part of this story, except it was midnight and no one was worried. Except I lived and Linda stayed eleven. I turn off the laptop before the story takes over. I look up at the trees that look windy and worried.

Dear Eleven-Year-Old Linda,
  I feel you.

I carry her to the sink like a prayer and cup my hands under water. I wash my face and check the mirror. I am her for now. This is what it's like to love the drowned. You carry them around and channel each other. You ask yourself, why am I here and why not there?

Maybe every rape story told out loud in the world is a carefully placed mirror for something gone missing.

~~~

WE DO *all we can. We can, to survive.*—Elizabeth Smart

Even then, what are the odds? Some would say slim, some would say Stockholm syndrome.

[It] is not a syndrome. It is a survival strategy.—Natascha Kampusch

Natascha Kampusch—an Austrian woman, kidnapped at ten years of age and held in a hell of a basement for eight long years.

Kampusch describes how her captor starved her and beat her, then stood her naked one midnight at the threshold of his home when she was a teen and dared her to run. She knew what I knew when I got small in the truck—no one will help me, and this will get worse. Her captor laughed as she froze in the doorway. *See how the world doesn't want you anymore?*

When the conditions were just right, she made her escape and returned to the world. Then half the world asked why she hadn't run sooner.

This is what it is when we surface alive—they don't see us as champions, and they don't see us as swimmers. They think we are hexed. *What happened to all the rocks wrapped around you?*

We carried the rocks. We are that kind of strong.

～～

A LAST-MINUTE rain has come and gone, and now another hot day is getting ready to end. I walk through the wet streets and look for the kind of cool that comes after a rain. I get the kind of steam exhaled from hot streets with nowhere to go. Still, this is the blue hour, and the blue hour is good. Credit the French who first named the hour. Credit the green tilt and turn at the end of the day.

Dark-purple leaves ripple over my head, and I pause on the sidewalk to watch as they flutter. They sound like little waves on the water. Something white catches my eye a few yards away. Something half in the mud. Maybe it's trash, though it looks like a book. Abandoned books are good luck to save and bad luck to leave. The least I can do is get it out of the mud. I can bring it to Goodwill and donate the merit.

I walk over, and the shape of a book comes sharp into focus. The book lies in a thin slip of mud by the side of the road. Elizabeth Smart's face is on the book's cover. Her name is in gold letters right under her photo. I stop for a minute and look at my hands.

Am I dreaming this? Is this really real? I feel my feet feeling wet inside my shoes. I feel here and now by the side of the road.

Where There's Hope, by Elizabeth Smart—in spite of the rain, offsetting the mud. What are the odds? The odds are so small.

I pick up her story, shake off the mud, and tuck it under my arm. I think of the 800, forgotten and not famous. I inhale the odds and exhale the sparrows as I walk back to my place and sit on the stoop. The hour is ending. A few bruised clouds float overhead. And there, in the bottom of the sky, the evening's first star shines like a flashlight, all the way through infinity, for everyone to see.

ACKNOWLEDGMENTS

TO THE MANY PEOPLE who helped me learn to read and write and find my voice and encouraged me to keep on keeping on, you have revealed to me the surprising gifts of interdependence. Thank you.

I am deeply grateful to:

Claire Anderson-Wheeler, my brave agent whose vision and heart brought this book to light. And her colleagues at Regal Hoffmann & Associates.

Cate Hodorowicz and the rest of the extraordinary University of North Carolina Press team who made a home for my work. I am a fortunate one.

The writers who have nurtured my words, specifically, and in order of appearance—Georgann Eubanks from the start; Lynn Otto, who always encouraged more poems; Phillip Shabazz, whose generosity and talent astound me; and the remarkable Abigail DeWitt, who saw what I could not see and never stopped seeing it.

The talented and joyful writers and teachers at Table Rock Writing Workshop. And writing groups everywhere who provide support to writers of every stripe.

The many teachers and guides who've encouraged me along the way, specifically Geshe Gelek Chodha, Frank L. Daggs, Linda G., Pam Hogan, LaVerne Kappel, and Jeanette, who taught me the art of the spy.

And my mother, to the moon and back.

Heartfelt thanks also to the editors and staff of the following literary reviews where portions of this book first appeared in different forms:

Bellevue Literary Review: "The Empath"

iamb, poetry seen and heard: "Small" and "Whereabouts"

Xavier Review: "Visitation"

~~~